THE VIEW FROM NINETY

ALSO BY CHARLES HANDY

The New Philanthropists (with Elizabeth Handy)
Myself and Other More Important Matters
Reinvented Lives (with Elizabeth Handy)
The Elephant and the Flea
Thoughts for the Day (previously published as *Waiting for the Mountain to Move*)
The New Alchemists (with Elizabeth Handy)
The Hungry Spirit
Beyond Certainty
The Empty Raincoat
Inside Organizations
The Age of Unreason
Understanding Voluntary Organizations
Understanding Schools as Organizations
The Future of Work
Gods of Management
Understanding Organizations
The Second Curve
21 Letters on Life and Its Challenges

THE VIEW FROM NINETY

Reflections on How to Live a Long, Contented Life

CHARLES HANDY

HUTCHINSON
HEINEMANN

HUTCHINSON HEINEMANN

UK | USA | Canada | Ireland | Australia
India | New Zealand | South Africa

Hutchinson Heinemann is part of the Penguin Random House group of companies whose addresses can be found at global.penguinrandomhouse.com

Penguin Random House UK,
One Embassy Gardens, 8 Viaduct Gardens, London SW11 7BW

penguin.co.uk

 Penguin Random House UK

First published 2025

003

Copyright © The Estate of Charles Handy, 2025

The moral right of the author has been asserted

The essays in this book first appeared in the *Idler* magazine between 2020 and 2024. Some have been lightly edited for book publication to avoid the occasional repetition of ideas inevitable in articles that appeared over a four-year period. The publishers would like to express their gratitude to the editor of the *Idler* for his help and support.

Penguin Random House values and supports copyright. Copyright fuels creativity, encourages diverse voices, promotes freedom of expression and supports a vibrant culture. Thank you for purchasing an authorised edition of this book and for respecting intellectual property laws by not reproducing, scanning or distributing any part of it by any means without permission. You are supporting authors and enabling Penguin Random House to continue to publish books for everyone. No part of this book may be used or reproduced in any manner for the purpose of training artificial intelligence technologies or systems. In accordance with Article 4(3) of the DSM Directive 2019/790, Penguin Random House expressly reserves this work from the text and data mining exception.

Set in 14.2/17.4pt Garamond Premier Pro
Typeset by Jouve (UK), Milton Keynes

Printed and bound in Great Britain by Clays Ltd, Elcograf S.p.A.

The authorised representative in the EEA is Penguin Random House Ireland, Morrison Chambers, 32 Nassau Street, Dublin D02 YH68

A CIP catalogue record for this book is available from the British Library

ISBN: 978–1–529–15480–1 (hardback)
ISBN: 978–1–529–15481–8 (trade paperback)

Penguin Random House is committed to a sustainable future for our business, our readers and our planet. This book is made from Forest Stewardship Council® certified paper.

To Liz, who expected great things of me but never explained what they were.

CONTENTS

Introduction   1

PART 1: YOUR LIFE

1. It's OK to Go the Wrong Way   7
2. Don't Try to Explain Everything   10
3. The Pleasures of Solitude   13
4. On Being Wrong   16
5. Beware Wilful Blindness   20
6. The Truth About Comb-overs   23
7. Find Your Flaws   27
8. Just Listen   29
9. The Wisdom of Uncertainty   32
10. What Luck Is   37
11. The Deadly Dangers of Hubris   39
12. What's the Meaning of Success?   43
13. The Bishop, the Stoics and Me   46
14. The Greatest Painting in the World   50

PART 2: THE LIVES OF OTHERS

15. What's Important to Italians   57
16. How Young Women Are Changing the World   59
17. The Importance of Friendship   63
18. Drains and Radiators   68

CONTENTS

19. The Chinese Contract	71
20. Get Past Stereotypes	74
21. Don't Fence Yourself In	77
22. The Origins of Boxing Day	80

PART 3: WORKING LIFE

23. Two Types of Freedom	85
24. Fees or Wages?	89
25. The Joys of Self-Employment	92
26. Goodbye Nine-to-Five; Hello Oxford Hours	96
27. Rethinking the Working Week	98
28. Is Kindness An Asset in Business?	100
29. The Power of the Humble	104
30. My Grandson and the Marines	107
31. The Importance of Leaving Well Alone	110
32. My Fantasy Office	113
33. Grow Better, Not Bigger	118
34. My New Business Idea	121

PART 4: EVERYDAY LIFE

35. The Power of Names	127
36. The Rise of Empathy	130
37. Why Ownership is a Trap	133
38. Personality vs Character	136
39. The Joy of Teaching	138
40. The Past Won't Help the Future	140

CONTENTS

41. Let's Do Away with Dichotomies — 143
42. Why Differences Make a Difference — 146
43. Happiness, the Chinese Way — 150
44. The Narcissus Syndrome — 151
45. What Does 'Fair' Mean? — 154
46. A Thought on Ritual — 156
47. How to Say Thank You — 158
48. Who Is God? — 160

PART 5: LIFE AND DEATH

49. What Fun It Is Getting Old — 167
50. A Letter to God — 171
51. Inventing a New Life — 175
52. A Poem to Learn Before You Die — 177
53. Breaking Good — 180
54. What Would They Write on Your Tombstone? — 184
55. The Stoics and the Christians — 187
56. Preparing for the Inevitable — 190

Acknowledgements — 195

INTRODUCTION

I WOKE UP one morning to a rainy but intermittently sunny day. Nothing unusual about that you may say. Except that for me it was, because I was supposed to be dead. When I recovered from my stroke a few years ago, they told me it was highly probable I would suffer another stroke, this time fatal, within a further two. So to wake up in the morning and open my eyes and realise I was still alive was a great surprise, and I thought with relief, 'Not ready yet.'

So there I was, statistically dead. The same may soon be true of many of you. At any rate, some of you will be, as I am, old. I'm now over ninety, and though disabled because of the stroke, I'm otherwise raring to go and enjoying life – probably too much.

As I walk through the Valley of the Shadow of Death, as the Bible puts it, I've had plenty of time to meditate and reflect on my life. And, on the whole, I'm well satisfied. There are things I could have done that I didn't, but only a few things I did that I shouldn't have – for which I have made my apologies to the people concerned and forgiven myself for the mistakes I have made.

Although my work – writing books – was moderately successful, what I'm most proud of is my family, my son and my daughter, who, despite a woeful lack of good parenting, have somehow emerged as very nice, decent people: kind, interesting, fun to be with, good at their jobs and amazing in their ability to take care of me as an extra child. I'm very proud of them and very grateful, and I regard this as my greatest success in life, even though I had little to do with it. It was my late wife who dominated as a matriarch, who built four fabulous family homes, organised my life and would have liked to organise theirs if they'd let her.

Anyway, there we are; a life much enjoyed, probably too well lived in some respects. And now, how fortunate I am to have been given these few months at the end of it, to walk that valley and linger a while with the memories of what was but no longer can be.

And looking at the statistics it seems that, as the decades pass, there will be more and more old people around. Will that be good or bad? I wonder. I'd like to think it will be good, but looking at myself as an old man, I'm not so sure. I'm still very cantankerous, but now I use old age as the authority for my views, as my right to trample on the evidence of views that don't agree with

INTRODUCTION

mine. What will the next century be like? Full of cantankerous old folk like me, or peopled by quieter, more peaceful individuals? Will there be more book clubs or more raves? More old ladies riding bicycles upright and slow, as the Dutch do, or crouched down and speedy?

I have ideas these days, but I don't have the physical energy to do anything about them. And therefore they linger, undone in my mind. We need young people to make things change and old people to let them change. I hope I'll be more tolerant than I have been lately.

So may I pass on to you my Irish blessing, which I love. It goes like this:

Wherever the journey of life may take you,
May the road rise up to meet you as you go,
And the wind be always at your back.
May the sun shine warm upon your face,
And the rain fall soft on your fields.
And until we meet again, sometime, somehow, somewhere,
May God hold you in the palm of His hand and keep you safe.

Enjoy life. Don't leave it all too late.

PART I
YOUR LIFE

I

IT'S OK TO GO THE WRONG WAY

MY FRIEND RAJI emailed me. 'We have a new saying in Mumbai, Charles,' he wrote. 'I thought you might like it. It goes like this: "Sometimes the wrong train leads you to the right destination."' No, he wasn't talking about the chaotic railway system in Mumbai; he was talking about life and fate. And I knew from my own life exactly what the saying meant.

When I left university, I was determined to secure a good long-term job, and to earn enough money to support a family. I applied to Shell International oil company. My parents didn't really approve of my decision but they made no comment and when I left to go to my first posting in Singapore, my mother drove me to the airport. I looked miserable and a bit apprehensive so she wound down the window as I left and said to me, 'Never mind, dear, it'll all be great material for your books.'

'Books, Mother?' I said. 'I'm off to be an oil executive and get rich.'

'Yes, dear,' she said, in a kind, disapproving tone.

So off I went to Singapore where they posted me to Borneo to run their marketing company in Sarawak, surrounded by jungle and rivers.

I wasn't very good as a manager, so in the end I went and bought a load of management books, all American, and sat down to study them. I was appalled at how badly written they were, and how boring. I decided I could write them much better.

I took parts of them, the theories, copied them down, and wrote them out in my best English (I thought I was a pretty good writer, modelling myself on Ernest Hemingway, with short snappy sentences). And I illustrated it all with exotic stories of my time in Borneo, most of which was pretty disastrous, but as I said to the readers: you only learn by making mistakes, and as it's so much better to learn from somebody else's mistakes than your own, here are mine . . .

The book was surprisingly successful. It sold 10,000 copies in the first month when it came out and went on to sell 1,000,000 around the world by the end of the year. I then got requests from other publishers to write more books and so I became a writer. I also went around the world talking about the ideas in the book to endless groups of business executives, for which they paid me a lot of money.

So I ended up doing what I love doing, writing and telling stories, and being paid for it.

With that in mind, I wrote back to my friend in India and said, 'I got on a train that I hoped was going to lead me to Shell International but instead it took me to Penguin and the BBC, and Souvenir Press and to a life that I love and seem to do quite well at. Thank you very much for your Mumbai saying. I will pass it on to my grandchildren.'

So to my grandchildren I say this: experiment in your twenties before you have a family and a mortgage, because then if you fail it doesn't matter and you'll learn a lot from your mistakes. Get on whatever train you think might be interesting and see where it takes you.

2

DON'T TRY TO
EXPLAIN EVERYTHING

WHEN I WAS young I asked my mother about some of the more fantastical aspects of the Bible. 'Darling, just believe – you don't have to have reasons,' she replied.

'But I do,' I insisted. 'I need evidence. I need logical reasons for how these things could happen. You've asked me to believe five impossible things before lunchtime and given me no facts, no reasons – I can't do that.'

She shook her head sadly.

In time, I learnt to suspend my search for reason and facts. Why on earth not just let the canticles of evensong, the words of the Bible and the prayer book, the beautiful architecture of the cathedral and the music of Mozart or whoever, seep in? Don't try to explain it, just accept it.

These days, I've even stopped trying to bully people out of those beliefs they can't defend. I now think it's grossly rude to do such a thing. People are allowed to believe what they want to believe. After all, I don't quarrel with my grandchildren when they say they see little people bouncing up and down on the branch of a tree in the back garden: magic has its place.

Artists, poets and children see the world in a different way. I think many entrepreneurs similarly have an ability to believe in a new, invented product or service without necessarily being able to explain exactly why it will work. Take Dr Spencer Silver, for instance – the man without whom we would not have Post-it Notes.

A scientist working at US multinational conglomerate 3M, Silver tried to develop a super-strong adhesive, but instead accidentally created a 'low-tack', reusable, pressure-sensitive adhesive. He believed his invention would have some kind of practical use but didn't know what exactly.

Then a colleague came up with the idea of using the adhesive to anchor his bookmark in his hymn book. And soon they came up with this piece of paper that sticks but doesn't stick too much.

Which actually proved a hard sell to the bosses at 3M.

'What will people use it for? How will we market it?'

When they eventually did make their first yellow sticky Post-it Notes, everybody intuitively recognised what they were for. But you couldn't have explained exactly how useful they would be: people had to use them in order to see for themselves.

So, if you see people in your organisation dreaming away, let them do it, and savour what they come up with, without too many queries. It isn't always polite to ask the cook exactly how he or she made that delicious fish soup – just eat and enjoy. Sometimes knowing too much can spoil things.

Cultivate your own alternative capability, your imagination. And don't keep it to yourself – use it to create something, whether it's a film, a book or a product. You don't need to explain everything to everyone, or even to yourself. And believe. Yes, believe you can do these things.

3

THE PLEASURES OF SOLITUDE

THE REAL MEASURE of success in Britain is to be invited to be a guest on *Desert Island Discs*. It is a very strange form of success if you think about it, since the idea behind this radio programme is that you are choosing music you would listen to if you were a solitary castaway on a desert island.

Well, it never happened to me in Britain, but I did do the equivalent programme in Australia. There is nothing bad about an Englishman – or rather, in my case, an Irishman – being a success in Australia but not in his own country. However, it was strange that the last time I went to Melbourne, nobody seemed to notice me when I was there.

And I have to tell you, if you want to feel lonely, try turning on the evening television news in a strange country. You cannot imagine what all these funny people are doing and why they are worried about what's appearing on the screen. You feel very alienated and long for the sight of Big Ben and the face of the UK prime minister to reassure you that life is going on, or life as you understand it anyway.

I, however, am lucky. I quite enjoy my own company, and I relish the opportunity to ponder the questions so many of us tend to ask ourselves. You know, why are we living? Is death something to be worried about? Does God exist?

My wife couldn't understand my predilection for musing. 'Why don't you try living, instead of just talking about it? Go and cook something for us.' Well, cooking is something we were both very interested in. In fact, cookery books, well-illustrated, were our form of gentle pornography. We loved leafing through them and thinking about them, so long as we weren't expected to actually cook anything that they showed. And if conversation dried up between us, we could always debate the merits of Burgundy as opposed to Bordeaux wines and even try a little private tasting between ourselves. Very interesting and educational. And, in fact, a form of musing.

Now that I have had a stroke and am disabled, I am effectively a prisoner in my own home. I tolerate it. No, I don't just tolerate it, I enjoy it. As I said, I am my own best company. There is always somebody to grumble

THE PLEASURES OF SOLITUDE

with about life and its unfairness; always someone to complain to about other people, and always someone to test out my ideas on, even if they always agree with me.

Actually, that's not quite true – my best friend doesn't always agree with me, and that's what makes him interesting. Sometimes, in fact, I think he's more interesting than me, and I would like to be him.

I suppose that's why I'm such a fan of idleness. It's just another excuse to hide away with my friend while we solve the problems of the world and have a quiet drink of red wine while we do it.

4

ON BEING WRONG

IN AUGUST 1650, the Lord Protector of England, Scotland and Ireland, Oliver Cromwell, wrote to the stubborn elders of the Church of Scotland, saying: 'I beseech you, in the bowels of Christ, think it possible that you may be mistaken.'

Nearer home, we professors in the department of the university where I used to teach were asked to approve the elevation of Harris (as I will call him) to our fraternity, the professoriate. Harris was an acknowledged expert in his subject, well respected around the world. In person, he was a walking encyclopaedia who thought he knew everything. He even had the effrontery to lecture me on my subject, 'The Future of Work', and my wife on how to cope with the pains of childbirth. She was not amused.

Doubt was not part of his make-up. And that, in my view, was a problem. The thing is, to be a proper professor, you need to have decent doubt. Decent doubt is the foundation of all science. You challenge the state of knowledge as it exists and try to move it on. The fundamental requirement of all teachers is to display reasonable doubt – to be open to argument, even from your students.

Decent doubt, as Oliver Cromwell tried to remind the Scottish elders, is the foundation of religion, for without the doubt, you would not need faith. Decent doubt is at the heart of everyday companionship. You cannot have a discussion with somebody who does not concede that they might sometimes be open to being disagreed with.

It can be hard to live with someone who has no decent doubt. My late wife, whom I miss very sadly, seldom acknowledged doubt.

She trusted her instinct. 'I think with my guts,' she said. 'And they are always right.'

In my arguments with her, which were many, I believed I could triumph easily, having been trained to reason by endless writing of essays.

Unfortunately for me, she was one of those rare people who are normally right, while I was generally wrong.

When I was talking to her, I often had to doubt my own reasoning powers. Thenceforth I decided: 'My job is to work out why my wife is right and I am not.

That way we can both share in the decision.' I came to acknowledge that she was an exception to the rule of decent doubt.

In other areas of my life and in my teaching, though, doubt has proved an important component. When I was a teacher, I would endlessly tell my management students that good management is essentially common sense. The trouble is, common sense is neither common nor often sensible. You have to challenge it, you have to doubt it.

So when you think you've got a solution, assume that it could be better, doubt that it is right. And discipline yourself to choose at least another two possible answers, to test it.

You will make yourself much more agreeable as a workmate or as a boss, and far more agreeable as a conversationalist and a friend.

Decent doubt is a form of strength because it goes with modesty and a sense of humility. It would be nice if our politicians exhibited some decent doubt when they go on the television or the radio, and could admit that perhaps they are not always right, and perhaps things could be improved on.

So my recommendation to you is, even when you are absolutely sure that you are right, admit at least privately, and preferably publicly, that you could be wrong.

It makes you more approachable, more lovable, more friendly, more acceptable, more believable.

And you need to practise what I preach, just as I had to learn to practise it myself when confronted with my wife's infallible instinct and intuition.

5

BEWARE WILFUL BLINDNESS

I WAS LYING in bed looking at the ceiling when I noticed a brown stain in one corner. 'Oh, dear,' I thought. 'My neighbour above has got a leak somewhere. What a nuisance.'

It wasn't the money (the insurance would cover that), it was the hassle I dreaded. And the negotiations. He was a difficult guy.

So I shut my eyes, got up, got dressed and went about my work. Perhaps in the hot weather it will dry out, I told myself. After that I put all thought of it to the back of my mind.

Alas, when I went to lie down in the afternoon, the stain was still there. 'Oh, dear,' I thought again. Then I shifted my gaze to the rest of the ceiling which was mercifully clear of any stains. Then I forgot about it, for the time being. Do something about it tomorrow? Perhaps.

I was indulging in what is called *wilful blindness*, a reluctance to face up to awkward facts or bad news. The concept was coined by Margaret Heffernan, a wise and witty writer on work and management.

Once you've got the concept in your head, you see its various manifestations everywhere. I have two athletic friends: one is a keen rugby player, the other a boxer. Both seem to be impervious to all the statistics on the dangers of their sports. Somehow they feel they are invincible.

Another friend visited the other day. He had just received a report from the surveyors on a property he was longing to own.

'Is it good or bad?' I asked. He said, 'I haven't looked, they are always bad. These people, they make it worse than it is just in case they get sued. So I never pay any attention to them.'

'Oh, well,' I thought. 'It's his money, not mine.'

But that reminded me of the stain on my ceiling. I went to have a look. It was still there. 'Oh, well, give it another week,' I decided, and went back to work. Wilful blindness shown by both of us.

You see it everywhere: governments opt to ignore the alarming rise in the balance of payments deficit, or the signs of an impending disease.

The number of times I've heard people say, 'Oh, it will pass, don't worry,' when somebody is ill and suffering pain. I do it myself. 'Oh, it's just a cold,' I say. 'I'll take a pill.' Ignoring the alarming pains in my stomach. Most doctors are well aware of wilful blindness, particularly amongst men.

'I am sure we can all think of instances in our own lives, like my ceiling stain, where we don't want to face up to reality. And so we shut our eyes and hope it will go away.

Wilful blindness is prevalent throughout society but particularly in business and in management circles.

If you notice it in your own life, shut it down. It can be very dangerous.

I never did face up to my neighbour about the leak and I haven't looked at the stain for weeks, but I suspect it's still there. Sometimes the blindness is deliberate, sometimes it's my subconscious acting on my behalf, keeping me from getting worried. Either way, it is a dangerous lapse of concentration.

And, to be honest, it can be cowardice . . . in my case, always.

6

THE TRUTH ABOUT COMB-OVERS

MY MOTHER USED to say to me, 'Always tell the truth – it'll make life simpler. And if you don't, the truth will come back to bite you.'

I soon found out how wise she was. At the age of thirty-three, I found I was going bald. Well, a bit of me was, but with careful use of the comb, I could get a tuft of hair to cover my bald patch. And provided I didn't go out in the wind and held my head at the right angle, no one would know. Except my very bossy neighbour, the wife of a canon at Windsor, a kind soul but quite tough. One day she invited me to tea – and set about me.

'Charles,' she said, '*you* know you're bald, we *all* know you're bald. There's nothing shameful about being bald at your age, lots of people are. But what's shameful is trying to pretend you're not by careful use of your comb. You deceive nobody, you make yourself a laughing-stock – don't do it. Go downtown to the barber, get him to cut off that offending bit and be your honest self. You'll find it a great release once you get used to it.'

Well, she was a fierce old lady so I really had no choice. I went to the barber's and had my quiff cut off. And there I was – bald as a coot except for just above my ears.

It took me a long time to get used to it, but I had to admit, it did make life simpler. When I got out of the swimming pool, I didn't need to dry my hair, I just wiped my head like I did the rest of my body and the sun did the rest. It shortened time spent getting ready in the morning as I didn't have to brush my hair.

Plus, after a while anyway, I felt I was being true to myself. I was no longer pretending to be someone I wasn't. And do you know what? Nobody seemed to notice the difference. It made me feel free.

The next thing that happened was I went to get my eyes tested. And it was like an exam – they kept putting letters up in front of me and asking me to read them. Well, I couldn't see them very well so I tried guessing.

Eventually the optician lost patience. 'Look,' he said, 'I know you're lying. I know you're pretending you can see the letters. But sometimes you might guess the right one, which will give me a false reading of your eyesight. Unless you tell me the truth, I can't prescribe the right lenses for your glasses and so you won't be able to see as well as you could.'

I accepted he was right and I started telling him the truth. I got my glasses and I could see again.

So telling the truth not only made me feel freer, it also helped me see better.

And then there was my building project. Now, I knew from experience that if a builder tells you it will cost X and be done in Y, well, you can usually just about double both of those quantities. So this time I said, 'Please, give me the real quote – the one that includes all the things that could go wrong – and once I get over the shock, we can work together in harmony and produce a good result. Otherwise we'll end up quarrelling – you'll say it can't be done that cheap and I'll say you're over-charging me.'

He gave me what he thought was a true cost and a true timing and I was shocked. But once I got over the pain, we worked together very well. And would you believe it? In the end it came in slightly below cost and slightly earlier than expected. So the truth really worked in my favour again.

The same applies if you're leading any kind of team, whether on the sports field or at work. You have to tell the truth and get everybody else to tell the truth. If they don't, you can't trust them, and trust is the lubricant that keeps the world running smoothly. Without it everything gets jammed.

Yes, telling the truth is essential within the family and at work. In fact, truth heads the list of Aristotle's virtues, followed by courage, by which he means the moral courage to stand by what is right, whatever the consequences.

So take my mother's wise advice and don't let the truth come back to bite you.

7

FIND YOUR FLAWS

MANY YEARS AGO when I was in my early twenties and working for Shell, I was responsible throughout a whole day for all the oil refuelling at Singapore international airport.

It wasn't quite as difficult as you might think; everything was foolproof – it was colour-coded. All I had to do was fasten the red hose to the red valve on the plane's tank and the green hose to the green tank.

But these hoses are quite difficult to lug around. It was a hot day and somehow I got muddled. 'You damned fool! Are you colour blind?' the supervisor shouted at me.

I was shocked. It was like being asked in public if I had syphilis. I said, 'No, of course not!' But he was right. Although I didn't know it at the time, I couldn't distinguish green from red. Of course, Shell should have tested me before asking me to do anything like that, but they didn't.

So what else do I not know about myself? I wonder. What about you, are you colour blind? Or is there some aspect of your body or your personality that you are unaware of? Are you hyperactive? Or partially deaf? Ask your best friend.

We don't know everything about ourselves, and that can be dangerous, as it was with me. The wrong fuel would have caused engines to stall. Planes would have dropped from the sky.

Even today, sitting in an aeroplane waiting for it to take off, as the engines start up, I listen acutely, hoping that whoever is doing my old job is not colour blind. Only when they're firing perfectly do I relax.

Your unknown flaws can be dangerous. Find them out before it's too late.

8

JUST LISTEN

I WAS TALKING with the theatre director Declan Donnellan, founder of Cheek by Jowl. I asked him what the secret was to being a great director. I hoped that his answer might give me some clues as a teacher.

He said, 'Pay attention! Not to the text of the play but to the individual actors. If one is having difficulty, you should take them aside.'

Paying attention, Declan said, does not mean telling them what to do. It means listening, but listening plus. It means doing your best to get inside their world. To get them to talk to you.

I love the piece of research which shows that the more you talk, the less you hear.

And the more you talk, the more highly you think of the person you are talking to, the listener. In other words, both sides gain – hopefully, the listener gains from listening to you, but you gain from perceiving his or her appreciation.

Paying attention is listening plus – that is, making someone feel they are the best person you've ever met.

There's a story of a young woman who was sent to interview two people running for President of the United States, some years ago. I think they were Bush and Clinton but I'm not sure, so let's call them A and B.

She said, 'When I was talking to A, I felt it was extraordinary to be in the same room with the most powerful man in the world.

'But when I was with President B, it was extraordinary to feel that I was the most important woman in the world, because he was paying attention.'

We had Dutch friends who had what we regarded as a brilliant family. There were three teenage kids who were mature, charming, interesting, able to talk freely and engage with us. And we compared our own kids unfavourably with them.

We said to our Dutch friends, 'How do you do it? What is the secret?'

'We treat each child as if it were an only child,' they said. 'We make sure that once a month, we take each of them out on their own somewhere and listen to them, pay attention to them, and try to get inside their mind and their world.'

This obviously pays huge dividends.

So don't tell, listen. Listen plus. It is a lesson that

most managers could learn. Don't go around barking at people. Sit down and listen to them. You will gain their respect and they will be very appreciative of your wisdom in taking the time out to listen to them.

When anyone is going to an interview I say, 'Try and get the interviewer to talk more than you do. Keep asking them questions.' Because the research shows that the more the interviewer talks, the more favourably he or she views the interviewee.

Similarly, if you are at a dinner party and at a loss for what to say, turn to the neighbour on your right and say, 'Tell me . . .' and ask them some question. And they will think you are wonderful because you have the wisdom to listen to them. And you might actually learn something too.

9

THE WISDOM OF UNCERTAINTY

CAPABILITY IS A long and ugly word, particularly when it's attached to your name, as it was to the great landscape gardener Lancelot 'Capability' Brown. Apparently, he would look at the scene before him of pastures and untidy meadows and so on, and would say it had 'great capabilities' – by which he meant potential.

It's the same feeling I think that teachers must have when they walk into their classrooms in a primary school and look at all these potential geniuses. They must think to themselves, 'Wow, this place is full of capabilities.' Even if the pupils aren't capable at that particular moment of writing their names, it is all about potential.

So what on earth was Keats talking about when he wrote a letter to his brothers advocating 'negative capability'? That sounds like a contradiction. But he didn't mean it that way; he meant to be able to carry on even when, as he put it, 'being in uncertainties, mysteries, doubts, without any irritable reaching after fact and reason'. In other words, he was saying, facts get in the way of your imagination.

When I was about to take my final exam at Oxford, I asked my tutor if he had any hints about revision. He said, basically, don't.

'You don't need memory for this. They're not testing your memory. Surprise the examiners. Don't tell them what they already know, tell them something they hadn't thought about. So you need to go into the hall with an empty mind. The best thing you can do is go and lie on your back and listen to a cricket match. It's a very boring game but, you know, the click of ball on bat, the ripples of applause after a boundary or a maiden over, are the soothing music of an English summer's afternoon and they will effectively clear your mind of anything else. And when you've got a clear mind, your imagination goes at full pelt. If you require a fact, it will stream into your head just when you need it, because, believe me, it's part of your deeper memory.'

So I did as he suggested and I lay on my back and listened to the cricketers, and as he said, my mind became empty. And the next day, I walked into the examination hall feeling I knew nothing but that that was all right. And, yes indeed, I got my degree, thanks to my vivid reinterpretations of history and philosophy. I've been very grateful to cricket ever since, although I never played the thing.

Keats found he couldn't write poetry at all until he'd emptied his mind of any kind of fact or certainty. I find the same. Instinct can be powerful. My late wife always said her brain was in her gut; she knew by intuition. She said, 'I'm just as clever as you but in a different way.'

So if we came to a fork in the road, she would say, 'Go left,' and I would say, 'Why?', and she'd reply, 'I just feel it's right.'

After a bit I learnt to respect her instinct. And to make it acceptable to me, I used, as a kind of game, to work out some reasons why her instinct might possibly be right. As long as I could justify it to myself, I would go with it. And she was always right even if she couldn't explain why.

On one occasion I gave her facts. She didn't want to know; it mucked up her instinct. She was a photographer and a very creative, imaginative one. To her, truth was about seeing the real person, capturing that in some way. To do that she had to focus intensely on the subject and not concentrate too much on the particulars of the camera or the little focusing devices and so on. She had to rely on her instincts.

THE WISDOM OF UNCERTAINTY

It worked for her, and it worked for us. I gave free rein to her gut feelings, whether while buying a house or choosing a restaurant. The number of restaurants we walked out of because she said, 'It's not good, I don't want to eat here, it doesn't feel right.'

Trying to choose a school for our children was hopeless! I'd look up all the facts, the grades, sports records and so on; she'd walk into a classroom and say, 'No, I don't want my daughter sitting here, we won't go to this school.' And I could not convince her with facts.

So, negative capability! Don't let facts get in the way of your imagination. And just remember – truth is beauty, beauty truth. It doesn't have to 'look' nice: mathematicians and physicists tell me that equations with a set of numbers and letters can be very beautiful if they encapsulate the universe in just a short phrase. Similarly, if I can find a story or a metaphor that encapsulates the idea I am trying to promote then I think it is beautiful as well as true. True in the sense of a carpenter saying a joint is true, that it fits, it works. And then it is beautiful. Truth is beautiful – but not if it gets in the way of imagination.

So just sit down and paint, write, compose, design, whatever. Let your imagination flow free. Oh, and if you have an examination coming up, make sure your mind is empty and you have a lot of energy. It worked for me. I hope it works for you.

Have a great weekend, watch some cricket, empty your mind.

10

WHAT LUCK IS

I DON'T BELIEVE in luck. Or rather, I believe you make your own luck. Someone said luck is preparation when it meets opportunity. The British generally downplay individual efforts by saying, well, it was all just luck.

Yes, I've been lucky enough. But then, to paraphrase the golfing maxim: the more I have practised, the luckier I have been.

Napoleon is believed to have said that the only quality he wanted his generals to have was to be lucky. By which, to my way of thinking, he meant they'd done the real preparation so that they were ready for whatever happened. Be prepared, as the boy scout said.

When I worked for Shell, I was an occasional member of their scenario-planning group. The idea was that we in the group would try to forecast some possible catastrophe – the closing of the Suez Canal, the political collapse of Saudi Arabia – and then gather groups of managers to war-game what Shell should do to solve the problems that resulted.

It's a very good discipline, to be prepared. I wonder how many of us have done a fire drill in our homes in the last few months, or any disaster planning?

About a hundred years ago, my wife and I took seriously the possibility that one of us might end up disabled. We decided to design our own private care home in an apartment in our existing house, which we did. And now I reside in it very comfortably with a resident carer looking after me and cooking for me, and with my daughter in the main apartment downstairs. All because we planned it years ago when we had time and money and patience and were fit and well. I couldn't do it now that I am suffering from the effects of a stroke and am, in any case, much older.

So when people tell me how lucky I am to have my accommodation, I say, well, yes, but we did plan for this very situation. (Though sometimes I just say yes, I am indeed lucky, as though it was nothing to do with me.)

In other words, be prepared. Do some disaster planning and then, hopefully, you'll be prepared if disaster comes.

It's something governments might bear in mind, too.

II

THE DEADLY DANGERS OF HUBRIS

BY A TRICK of fate, I was put into the Classics stream at my preparatory school without my being asked. The result was I grew up studying Greek and Latin. I learnt all about Greek myths and gods and their naughty behaviour, and quite enjoyed it. But I also read the great Greek tragedies which in ancient times were performed in the wonderful theatre at Epidaurus, every year, for the whole populace to watch and learn from because they were really lessons in morality.

Hubris, which we were taught translates as 'excessive arrogance', to the Greeks meant thinking of yourself as some sort of god, behaving way above your station. Naturally this was resented by the Greek gods so they managed to make sure that anyone guilty of hubris tripped themselves up. Sitting there as a child, reading these plays and watching some of them, I kept wanting to say, as one does in a pantomime, 'Oh, please don't do that,' because it was obvious what would follow.

So when Oedipus, having killed his father, decides he wants to marry his mother, everything in me sort of reached out to him and said, 'No, don't! You'll only come to ruin,' which of course he did. And so, supposedly, the population of Athens would learn that arrogance was not a good thing; hubristic behaviour leads to disaster.

A few years back, like many others around the world, I saw an act of monumental hubris play out on television as President Trump reached the end of his term of office in 2020. Again, everything inside me wanted to say to the man, for whom I had no sympathy, 'Please don't do it! We can all see what's going to happen. It won't work out well for you.' And sure enough, it didn't. He went on to lose an election that most sitting presidents could have expected to win. If only Trump had grown up like me, learning Greek tragedy, he might have been able to look at what he was doing and think twice before doing it.

Oedipus should never have married his mother; it was obviously going to go wrong; but nobody could reach out and tell him. Of course, Oedipus deserved what he got, but still, I just itched to warn him. And the same was true of the dear Donald. Of course he deserved what he got, but I did want to warn him at

THE DEADLY DANGERS OF HUBRIS

various stages, 'Look behind you – it's going to catch up on you.' Again, like a pantomime.

But it was no good me bellowing at the television – he took no notice, of course, and the gods struck him down. Hopefully we can all learn what we're supposed to from that, just as the ancient Greeks did from their tragedies – that hubris, thinking you're bigger than you are, is to be avoided; it always ends in trouble.

If we learn nothing else from Donald Trump, at least we learn that Greek tragedy still has something to teach us: hubris is bad and leads to disaster. So thank you, Donald, for the reminder, if we needed it. Should your children show any signs of hubristic behaviour, a touch of arrogance, thinking they're bigger than they are, remind them of what happened to Oedipus in the Greek tragedies. Or to Donald Trump in this modern tragedy.

The gods now had to decide what punishment was fitting for Donald Trump. They decided that he should be confined to his new home in Florida where he would be required to play a round of golf every day, no matter the weather. He could choose his opponent and make up his own rules. But he had to play one round every morning.

The thought was that he would then learn that life is no fun if your sole motivation is to win – it gets very boring. Maybe that would force him to change his ways and, in the nature of Greek tragedies, provide a lesson for us all. In the event, after four years of punishment, the gods gave Donald Trump a second chance. It's worth bearing in mind, though, that when it comes to hubris, second chances are rare.

12

WHAT'S THE MEANING OF SUCCESS?

IT WAS ANOTHER family supper conversation: what does success mean? My teenage grandson had no doubt as to the answer: a lot of money to buy a lot of things – cars, motorbikes, perhaps even a yacht. My granddaughter thought likewise and was already designing her dream house: fantastic bedroom for her, amazing bathroom, and of course a terrace overlooking the sea, all paid for by the money she would earn if she were successful.

'What about you, Gaga?' asked my grandson.

I said, 'Come with me, I want to see your grandmother's grave.'

What they didn't know was that when she died, a kind friend had sent some snowdrops to plant on top of the grave. I wanted to see how they were doing.

The grave is only a few hundred yards from our house, so we went there.

No snowdrops on the grave, but lots of them on

others. They'd emigrated. I didn't know snowdrops did that, but there they were on tombs – some belonging to friends and neighbours of ours – all over the graveyard, even over by the hedge on the lane beside it.

On a whim, I said to myself, 'I think these snowdrops are her friends.' My late wife loved people, loved photographing them, and had oodles of friends. She maintained constant touch with them. She would spend an hour on the phone to a friend, and I'd say to her, 'What was that about?'

'Oh, just stuff,' she'd say, 'keeping in touch.'

That was her 'watering and fertilising' her friendships, keeping the snowdrops healthy. She'd say to me, 'We've got nobody coming on Sunday – shall we ask the so-and-sos to lunch?' Well, I'd like them enough, so they'd come. And she would pour them my good wine with lots of love. And yes, some lived nearby, in the village, but some were far away, in all corners of the world – but still she kept in touch with them.

I said to my grandchildren, 'It's a lovely sight, isn't it? There she lies, surrounded by the snowdrops. You see, for your granny, friends were so important – and she knew that, just like you had to keep flowers watered and fertilised, you had to look after your friends, and show them care and love. So now at her end she's surrounded by her friends.

WHAT'S THE MEANING OF SUCCESS?

'So please keep in touch with your friends in life and show them love. And I hope that when you die, you too will be surrounded by snowdrops.'

My wife's greatest compliment to me was that she once called me her best friend. I was chief snowdrop – what a great privilege. What success.

My wife led a well-lived, well-loved life. And I can't think of anything more successful than that – more valuable than all the money in the world.

13

THE BISHOP, THE STOICS AND ME

I'VE ALWAYS MAINTAINED that, within human organisations, managing your relationships with the people above you is as important as managing your relationships with those at the same level as or below you. I haven't always been good at practising what I preach, as anybody reading my early reports from Shell would testify. My relationship with my last boss, some time ago now, and long after I had left Shell, was one of the most difficult.

He was a bishop, and also the Dean of St George's Chapel in Windsor Castle where I was running a most unusual think tank, which had no staff. Every weekend we would bring in forty of the most prominent people in Britain – people at the heads of their businesses or institutions – to debate and discuss big moral issues of the time. Things like 'What kind of growth is good?' or 'Does all growth help?', 'Has freedom gone too far – should we police and regulate the Internet and social media, and if so, how?'

We passed no laws but in the discussions – coming from our different positions, all of us of equal importance – we educated each other.

It was the insight of David Hume, the great Scottish philosopher, that truth emerges from arguments amongst friends. I call the principle self-education by discussion. It works very well, it's exciting, it's great fun, everybody enjoys it and everybody learns something.

Then the day came when I had to have a big discussion with my boss, the bishop, about the future of my ingenious think tank. I had big dreams for it. I wanted to invite a group of forty people from the next generation, in their early thirties, at the start of promising careers. I would offer them accommodation in Windsor Castle so that they could bring partners, and live there for up to a month.

I thought they would add a new dimension to the debates, that each generation present could inform and educate and learn from the other with their different perspectives, and that for the newcomers it would be a wonderful opportunity to make friends who would help them in their future lives. Plus it would add some excitement to life in the castle.

My boss was not impressed. I couldn't get him excited about the scheme. Eventually he said, 'I think we need some help here, so let's go to the chapel and pray together.' I thought, 'Oh, dear, he's calling in God on his side – now I *am* done for.' So we went into St George's Chapel, a magnificent place. It's been there a very long time – the heraldic banners of the Knights of the Garter hang over the choir stalls – and we sat above the altar, and he said the Serenity Prayer, as it's called. It went like this.

'Dear Lord, grant to Charles your servant the serenity to accept the things he cannot change, the courage to change the things he can, and the wisdom to know the difference.'

Clearly, he thought I didn't have the wisdom to understand that the things I wanted to do there were unattainable because they would involve a fundamental redevelopment of parts of Windsor Castle, which had not only been there for a thousand years but was very much Her Majesty the Queen's private residence, over which she exerted substantial control. So I would have to make my case to her – not an easy task.

In the end we agreed to postpone the discussions for another week. But when I left, I did some research – and I realised that the bishop had led me, through the Serenity Prayer, to the Creed of the Stoic philosophy which I was beginning to adopt.

It has changed my life, that prayer, and I commend it to you. This is how it goes again: *'Dear Lord, grant unto me the serenity to accept the things I cannot change, the courage to change the things I can, and the wisdom to know the difference.'* That is very much the Stoic Creed – influence what you can influence with your values, but if you can't, then have the resilience to live with what is inevitable. Don't try to change what can't be changed.

The Stoics believed that there is a benign force in the world, the *logos*, which directs the order of things in nature and in life. It's sometimes called fate, or the system, or sometimes God. They believed we should learn to go with its flow and that everything would work out well, provided we had the courage and patience to see it through and influence it when we could.

So I'm grateful to my boss for the lesson he taught me. And from then on, I kept my mouth shut unless I could see an opening where I could add value.

Of course, sometimes people fall into the trap of thinking their input will be of no value and so they say nothing. Please don't fall into this trap. As someone once said, the worst kind of people are the ones who don't act because they think it'll make so little difference: every little difference helps.

14

THE GREATEST PAINTING IN THE WORLD

IF BY ANY chance you're travelling at some point in the near future, I would urge you, if you go to Italy, to find your way across the mountains to a little town called Sansepolcro. It's just a nice ordinary Tuscan place, but go into the Museo Civico and you'll find what Aldous Huxley called the greatest painting in the world. It's a fresco entitled *The Resurrection* and was painted by Piero della Francesca, one of the great Renaissance artists. It shows Jesus Christ rising out of a stone tomb ready to ascend into Heaven. Around him sit a group of Roman soldiers who were meant to be guarding the tomb and awaiting orders but have clearly fallen asleep.

Christ is not awaiting orders. As he rises, he is looking down at me, sitting on a chair in front of him, the piercing gaze challenging me to do what he is doing. No, not go to Heaven, but to have a new life, only on Earth as it is in Heaven; to reinvent myself, to leave my old self behind and create a new life in the here and now.

My old life wasn't very good, I'm ashamed of it. I was very selfish, I didn't produce much. But then even Christ could in some ways be regarded as a failure. His teaching fell on many deaf ears. His band of followers was so small they could all fit around one table for their last supper together. He died the death of a common thief.

Yet he was able to reinvent himself in a new world, in a new life.

The challenge to me was: can I reinvent myself, create a new life?

I feel very deeply that this challenge applies to us all. The painting is an invitation to create a new version of ourselves, to do something different, to lose ourselves in a cause or a purpose that is bigger than us.

Selfishness doesn't work very well in the longer term. We can't be alone in the world and we have to think of other people – for our own safety and for theirs.

We're part of a bigger scene. Let us think bigger. Let us find a cause to which we can devote ourselves, or let us create one. 'Be the new Charles Handy,' that risen Christ says to me. And let's hope it'll be a less selfish one. Because finding a way to help other people is actually deeply satisfying. In a way, you could say that doing so is in itself being selfish. But it's 'good' selfishness because it benefits others.

So, yes, your business or your organisation could be that greater cause, depending on who is leading it and how they define its purpose. I think businesses only survive if they have a purpose beyond their own survival. If the only thing they're interested in is profitability, they'll probably fail. The businesses that succeed are the ones that have something people can devote themselves to.

I wrote a book once called *The Hungry Spirit* in which I said that in Africa, they say that people have two hungers. One is for the means of life: food and shelter, and even money. The other is for a purpose in life: why you bother to stay alive. Capitalism satisfies the first hunger, but it doesn't satisfy the second. The second requires leaders who give us a cause to which we can devote ourselves. And that seems to be what's lacking in society these days. It still is every person for him or herself.

If the recent pandemic taught us anything it was that society only works when it works together. And that means it too must have a cause bigger than itself. Is it going to be climate change? I sincerely hope it will be.

This is the challenge for our national leaders – to get us to put up with our temporary discomforts in the cause of something bigger than ourselves. Something that will benefit our grandchildren and great-grandchildren.

I urge you to do what I have done on many occasions recently – to go out and plant a tree. Even if you know you might never sit under its shade, you'll also know it will be there for your grandchildren or others to enjoy. It gives you a good feeling, doing something that's not for yourself to enjoy but for others. It may even help to save the climate system.

And please, don't forget: go to Sansepolcro and sit in front of the greatest painting in the world.

PART 2
THE LIVES OF OTHERS

15

WHAT'S IMPORTANT TO ITALIANS

MANY YEARS AGO, listening to the BBC's *Today* programme one morning, I heard that the Italian government had collapsed for the third time in two weeks. The presenter John Humphrys was interviewing an Italian journalist.

'This is very important for your country,' said Humphrys to the journalist.

'Yes,' said the Italian, 'it is very serious. But it is not important.'

Of course, every Italian understood why he said that, and I did too. Italian life revolves around the local community, the local town, where the police are stationed, where you pay your taxes and where you register if you are a resident or temporary resident.

What goes on in Rome is interesting, and serious, too: foreign relations, national taxation, and so on. However, the changing political set-up really is only interesting to those who specialise in such things. Most people can't be bothered.

You can see two women and a man busily arguing in the piazza in an Italian village. If you go close you discover they are talking about what they are going to have for Sunday lunch, not politics.

So in your life, what is important and what is just serious? I subscribe to the Italian belief in the importance of three things – the three Fs: Family, Friends and Food. Get those right, concentrate on those, and life will go on, whatever happens. I mean, look after your family, the bills can wait till next week – probably no one will notice if they are paid a day or two late.

Sunday lunch is an important event in every Italian family. The time when outsiders are welcome and distant members of the family are reunited. Only you can decide what in your life is important and what is merely serious.

Of course, you must attend to the serious things, but not necessarily immediately. They can usually wait until next week, when you've got a clear head. However, the important things must be attended to straightaway.

Family, Friends and Food. I apply this in my own life – the three Fs certainly get priority over the serious stuff. And that includes work – life has to be lived, not just paid for. I'll work when I'm feeling brighter, if you don't mind.

16

HOW YOUNG WOMEN ARE CHANGING THE WORLD

I HADN'T HEARD of the word 'opinionista', and I think of myself as a wordsmith. I love new words, but I'm not so keen on a word that doesn't appear in the *Oxford English Dictionary* or that I can't call up in a thesaurus. It's hard to pronounce, difficult to spell and, as my mother said, surely there are enough words in the works of William Shakespeare or the Bible to say what you want to say without having to invent new ones. She's right. This is an invented word, concocted to make the user sound clever.

Why can't they use simple English words like 'model' or 'example'? But nowadays it's the new term in business marketing. You are qualified to be an opinionista if you have 10,000 or more followers on social media, on any of the platforms. Then you'll probably be approached by a marketing executive who'll try to persuade you or bribe you to use some perfume or sit in some car in the hope that some of your 10,000 followers will buy their perfume or their car.

Well, I'm all in favour of new business ideas and this is a cheap way of getting new endorsements from famous people. But I prefer the models of the social activists. The two young women, for instance, who are leading new movements to change the world. They're called Malala and Greta. You will have read about them. They really are the star opinionistas.

In 2008, when Malala was eleven years old, the Taliban took control of the part of Pakistan where she lived. One of the consequences was that girls were no longer allowed to attend school; the Taliban decreed that females were needed solely to produce food and babies. Only boys could receive lessons, to learn to fight.

Later, as a teenager, Malala began to speak out about this injustice. The Taliban leaders said: will somebody get rid of this pesky schoolgirl, she's a nuisance. So one morning a Taliban soldier got on the school bus. He said, 'Who is Malala?' She stood up and said, 'I'm Malala,' and he took out his revolver and shot her in the head.

Luckily, he missed her brain, just. Her father turned up, whisked her off and put her on a plane to England, where doctors in Birmingham saved her life.

Once she was recovered she continued her

campaign, broadening her agenda to include all human rights for women – not just the right to an education but to a career, the right to choose her own husband, to go to university – and she travelled the world with her message. She received awards everywhere and ended up sharing the Nobel Peace Prize, the youngest Nobel laureate in history. She's had a film made of her life. She's every young girl's heroine, I think.

I have two teenage granddaughters. They're incredibly beautiful, quite cheeky, quite naughty, quite charming. I've said to their parents in the past, 'You better watch out, these two are going to be trouble for you later on.' But actually I was wrong – they're gold dust. They're our hope for the future. And their models are Malala and Greta.

Greta, seventeen, the climate activist from Sweden, had the courage to bring her message to the United Nations Climate Action Summit and faced down the corporate chieftains at the World Economic Forum in Davos, challenging them to get their act together and go green before it's too late.

These two are models for the new generation and they give me hope. If one day you read of mass protests outside schools in south London, you'll know that my granddaughter Scarlett has organised something, following Greta's example. Good for her.

I asked Google, was this a trend? And Google told me there are thousands of young girls campaigning in this sort of way. Opinionistas, all of them, changing the way the rest of us think.

My two granddaughters have appointed themselves guardians of my morality. They make sure I say the correct thing – if they hear me utter anything they think is racist or sexist, or even too right-wing, they jump on me like little terrier dogs and punish me. And they're pretty strict. I'm quite frightened sitting with them sometimes, but it has certainly changed the way I behave and the way I speak. And good for them.

So congratulate your young girls, tell them to encourage other people to be like them, for they are the only signs of hope that I can see in this gloomy time.

17

THE IMPORTANCE OF FRIENDSHIP

IN THE YEARS since I had my stroke, I've lived in solitary confinement in my own apartment. A very comfortable prison. But I have discovered, as if I hadn't already known, that in order to be fully myself I need other people, particularly friends, people who have known me a long time, and know me better than I know myself. They can remind me of who I used to be and who, I hope, I still am.

I remember reading somewhere, 'A good friend is someone who knows all the worst things about you and still wants to have lunch with you.' That sums up the relationship between me and David, my oldest and best friend, whom I first met at university fifty years ago. We meet for lunch once a month, taking turns to name the restaurant and pay the bill.

Over lunch we share our most awkward secrets, our failures and our few successes. After all, what's the point of succeeding if you don't have somebody to boast to?

David knows everything about me, including my worst faults and temptations. He's always there to help if he can. He's also a very distinguished doctor, so if I fall over he knows which specialist to turn to, which hospital, and that is incredibly useful. When I nearly died after my stroke, I was delighted but not surprised when I came round in a hospital in The Hague to see David standing by my bedside.

Alerted by my family, he had flown straight there to be with me. Of course, that's what I would have done if it had been him in the hospital bed and not me.

My favourite of Shakespeare's Sonnets is the one you may well have heard at marriage services. It goes like this:

> *Let me not to the marriage of true minds*
> *Admit impediments. Love is not love*
> *Which alters when it alteration finds,*
> *Or bends with the remover to remove.*
> *O, no! It is an ever-fixèd mark*
> *That looks on tempests and is never shaken . . .*

Actually, I think Shakespeare was talking about friendship, not romantic love. When he uses the word love here, please think of it as an affection between

THE IMPORTANCE OF FRIENDSHIP

brothers or sisters, or between really good friends. A relationship of total trust and total truth. In fact, I think that a good marriage always ends up as a marriage of true minds, as a marriage of friends, of partnership, trust and equality.

Though, as my late wife constantly reminded me, with friendship you are two individuals, together but with space in the togetherness to be yourself. She even carried that through to the design of our houses; she believed a good marriage requires one bed for togetherness, but two bathrooms and two workrooms or studies, so you can be yourself when you need to be. There must be space in the togetherness.

I think she was right. It certainly worked for us. To have a room of one's own, as Virginia Woolf put it, is essential in a marriage, no matter how many wonderful nights you share.

Nowadays I couldn't live without my friends, people who knew me before I was ill, who assure me I'm the same person they used to know long ago. Who share my memories of the old world that we inhabited, and with whom I can put the world to rights, even if nobody seems to notice.

We all know each other's birthdays, each other's children. We share a history and hopefully a future.

If you have friends like that, grapple them to you

with hoops of steel, or with at least a lunch every month. They are worth their weight in gold.

One of my favourite books is called *How Many Friends Does One Person Need?*, a very approachable academic work by Professor Robin Dunbar of Oxford University.

He studied groups of people, working groups, down the ages from our hunter gatherer predecessors to Roman legions, right up to Facebook groupings in modern life. And he maintained that, when we're younger, we can only have five best friends because our brains are too small to cope with any more. But as we get older and our brains get bigger, we can raise that to fifteen, which is the size of a good dinner party.

You then go up in multiples of fifteen until you get to 150, which is the absolute maximum that any normal human can cope with, in terms of relationships involved. That maximum became known as the Dunbar number by many organisations who design their project teams around the number 150.

In my experience that is too large. I think seven is the perfect 'younger' number. So seven sevens are forty-nine, and that's my maximum size for an organisational group. If I were to design my own organisation, it would all be in multiples of seven.

Seven is the perfect number: it gives you the capacity

THE IMPORTANCE OF FRIENDSHIP

to include the variety of skills and talents that you would need in any group, but it's also small enough that if you all remain in it, you could become great friends.

The best teams on the pitch, it seems to me, are always such good friends, intuitively knowing each other's whereabouts, and where to pass to, almost without looking.

I think the same applies at work: the best groups are friendship work groups. They like and know each other, can trust each other and help each other. So I encourage work groups to socialise after work, to know each other very well.

I also believe they don't need to have job titles because they all know what they are and what each other does.

One of the happiest 'work' places I know is a primary school. All the kids there are budding with happiness because they're all friends. I'm amazed that my grandchildren adore their schools. I said to them, 'When I was young, I hated school.' But they say, no, they love it, because that's where their friends are – and where your friends are, that's where you want to be.

So friendship is invaluable and I hope you have just the right number, certainly one best friend. And if you can't live with them, lunch with them.

18

DRAINS AND RADIATORS

MY WIFE AND I once amused ourselves by dividing our friends and acquaintances into two categories, drains and radiators. The radiators were the ones who warmed the atmosphere and made life increasingly pleasant. The drains did exactly as the word suggests – they drained us, leaving us exhausted. What was interesting, and unexpected, was who fell into which category.

Take Bill. He saw himself as God's gift to humanity but became increasingly a pain as we had to listen again and again to his tedious stories and his bad jokes. In fact, he became a bore and actually a drain. On the other hand, Tom, who hardly said a word, infused the place with his happy temperament and made us all feel better without seeming to say anything much. He was a typical radiator really; you don't notice radiators because they are painted the same colour as the walls but they change the whole atmosphere of a room. That was Tom. How did he do it?

DRAINS AND RADIATORS

Around the same time, I was having a conversation with a friend of mine who is a famous theatrical director. I said, 'What is the secret to being a director?' 'Oh,' he replied, 'it's just two words, "pay attention".'

And I thought, 'That is more about life than it is directing plays. That is exactly what Tom does: he pays attention.' When he visited, he seemed riveted by everything I said or what my wife said when she talked about her photography. Of course, I'd heard it all before, but he made her really glow and it was a pleasure to see her come alive. He did it without saying a word, just by looking and listening.

I try to copy Tom. But it is exhausting, listening, particularly if you are paying attention, really listening. I mean, reading this through to yourself and thinking about it is actually quite exhausting. If I send you to sleep, I don't apologise; it is just part of the nature of thinking and paying attention.

So, have fun deciding who is a drain and who is a radiator but don't tell them. They wouldn't understand. Then decide which you want to be. I am afraid it is quite possible you are a bit of a drain. I know that I go on too long with my little thoughts but actually I get some of my best ideas from listening to other people talk. If I really pay attention – and stop drinking more wine – I am frequently inspired.

On the other hand, sometimes I educate myself by talking. One of my heroes, on whom I model myself, is a chap called Peter Drucker, one of the great gurus of management thinking. He lived in California. 'Peter,' I once asked him, 'where do you get all your ideas from? You are full of wise thoughts.' 'Ah,' he said, 'I get them by listening . . . [long, long pause] to myself.'

At first I thought, 'What an arrogant old bugger!' And then I realised that is exactly what I do myself. Only I put it down to my Irish ancestry. The Irish have a saying: how do I know what I think until I hear what I say? And, funnily enough, you quite often find yourself saying very wise things, much to your own surprise.

So pay attention to yourself in your wildest moments: you may be talking words of great wisdom. You too could be a radiator just by paying attention to what other people are doing. And you might even educate yourself, if you pay attention to what you are saying. For how do you know what you think until you hear what you are saying? Try it.

19

THE CHINESE CONTRACT

FIFTY YEARS AGO, I was the branch manager for Shell in the South of Malaysia, in what the company referred to as the Malacca Branch. One of my duties was to finalise trading terms with our agents, the people who ran the service stations in my area. I had yet to negotiate the big one which was run by a gentleman named Ahong in Malacca, the picturesque town where I lived.

I was good friends with Ahong and I had no reason to think that there would be any problem. He knew the standard terms and he had given me no indication that he was going to argue. Still, the conversation had to be had. So I went along one afternoon to his light-filled office overlooking the sea. I went through everything with him. The Chinese are instinctive business people, so I knew I had to offer him something. I therefore extended his credit terms which he was very pleased about. But I refused to budge on the discounts I was prepared to give him on the sales made to him.

By the end of it all, we were both happy. We had each given a little and both got more or less what we wanted. We shook hands. He produced a bottle of brandy as well as some ginger ale and we toasted ourselves and our future prosperity together. And then I produced the official agency agreement that Shell required him and me to sign, about three pages of it, covered all over with the Shell emblem. I filled in the numbers we had just agreed and gave it to him to sign.

He looked at it, and he looked at me, and he said, 'What's this?' I replied it was the agency agreement that we'd discussed, and that he just had to sign it. He said, 'Well, I'm not so sure I want to sign that. It suggests to me that you think you have got a better bargain than I have and you want to use the law to enforce it. I see this as a breach of our trust.'

'I understand your point,' I said, 'and I will take it back to my bosses in Kuala Lumpur, but in the meantime I am required to get you to sign this. It is just a formality, a bit of Shell bureaucracy. It has nothing to do with your relationship with me. Of course I trust you.'

He said, 'In China, we don't use that sort of thing. We say any agreement that is going to last must please both of us. We must both feel that we've got what we want from it.'

I said, 'Well, that's right, and haven't we?'

THE CHINESE CONTRACT

He said, 'Yes, but when you produce this document, it looks as if you think you've got the better of me. Why should I trust you?'

I asked him not to let it interfere with our good relationship. So in the end, reluctantly, he signed it and I took it back to my bosses and told them what he'd said.

I thought of that Chinese contract every time I negotiated with my children about when they should eat their food or go to bed. I still think about it every time I have an argument with anybody about anything. If both sides think they've won, then they are more likely to reach an agreement.

And so 'give to get and trust' is my motto in life. It helped me build a very good marriage, I believe, and I think my wife would have agreed. Give to get, then trust. Don't rely on signatures or bring in the law. When you have to use a lawyer, something has gone wrong.

So, may you have a happy time without too many fraught negotiations. But if you do have an argument with anybody, make sure that they get out of it as much as you do. Then you should trust them. If you can't trust them, it means that they haven't got enough. So give them more.

Good luck. Trust breeds relationships and they're worth their weight in gold.

20

GET PAST STEREOTYPES

YEARS AGO I went to America, to Boston, to study for a further degree. For the first week, the twelve new students on the course would gather together for introductory sessions, the idea being that if we got to know each other, it would help us in this strange new world we all found ourselves in.

So we sat there talking about the timetable, and what we expected, where we came from, what we hoped to get from this course, and where we were heading. It was all most informative. After five days, the professor in charge said, 'Well now, you have all been with each other for nearly a week, I think it will be instructive to discover what you think of each other. So, take a piece of paper, write your name at the top and pass it around. And, each of you, write one or two words to describe your impression of the person whose name is at the top of each sheet.' I thought this was quite a dangerous exercise, but I had nothing to fear. Being a stranger in

GET PAST STEREOTYPES

the country I had said very little, and so I was confident I would get an empty piece of paper back.

Or so I thought.

No way! I read twenty comments under 'Charles Handy'. They said: arrogant, rude, supercilious, unkind, snob, upper-class, thinks he's better than us, and so it went on.

'They can't possibly be talking about me,' I said to myself. 'I know what has happened. They think, because of my accent, that I am an Englishman, and this is what they think they are like. They are labelling me with their stereotype of an Englishman.' I got so angry, I jumped up. I banged on the table and said, 'I am not an Englishman, I am an Irishman, do you hear me? I am Irish. The English conquered us or tried to. I dislike them as much as you do.'

Ever since then I have been very careful to make sure as soon as I can, in any new group, that I tell them that I am Irish, not English, otherwise all the faults that they dislike in the English are going to be heaped on me through no fault of my own. As for my fellow students, I said to them, 'Look, I know you judge me for my accent but try to listen to what I'm saying. I'm me, Charles Handy, forget where I come from. I am my own brand, I don't march under any other people's flags.' Over time, they learnt to like me (I hope) as me, not as Charles the

Englishman with a funny voice, or Charles the Irishman who wasn't very Irish either.

How successful have I been? I don't know, but at least my friends know who I am and don't become confused by stereotypes. And with other people, I try not to burden them with all my impressions that have been piled up over the centuries. I try to find out what they as individuals stand for, what their values are, and what they want to contribute to this world. And if I succeed, I seem to make a friend for life.

21

DON'T FENCE YOURSELF IN

I ALWAYS ASSUMED that privacy was one of the basic human rights. That was until I went to live in Italy, where we had a small part of a large condominium, a sort of private village, in Tuscany.

One summer, I came home exhausted after a long day in the sun to find a couple, who were obviously just married, standing in all their finery posing for a photograph on our small lawn.

I was affronted. How dare they? Seething with anger, I rushed inside to get a stick. My late wife, who was much nicer than me, shouted out, 'Don't be angry, they've just got married.'

'Maybe,' I replied, 'but they're standing on our lawn.'

I rushed out. The groom, who was much taller than me and spoke excellent English, said: 'I am sorry if you feel I am intruding but I can see that you're English and you may not be aware of the law in Italy.

'In Italy all the land belongs to everyone. You may

own it, but you can't prevent other people from walking on it.

'So, I am afraid we are here whether you like it or not. I am sorry if you feel that we are intruding, but that is the way it is in Italy.'

Meanwhile my wife was busy in the kitchen. When I returned, she said, 'I told you so. We must be nice to them. I'll slice some cake; you go and open the champagne.'

I did what I was told and prepared a tray of glasses, then went outside to help them celebrate. Even with the bride's rather broken English and my very broken Italian, we got on well – thanks possibly to the champagne.

We had a nice little party with many toasts and a lot of happiness. When they left, in very good humour, the bride invited us to Sunday lunch with her family in their home.

Now, in Tuscany, the family Sunday lunch is a great ritual, with at least five courses and many bottles of the local Chianti. So for a foreigner to be invited to join one is a great honour, and I quickly accepted. After all, it would be wonderful to get to know another local family.

We went along that Sunday, and it turned out the bride's father was the local police chief – a very useful connection for the future. And of course the lunch itself was marvellous. All in all, it was a great success.

DON'T FENCE YOURSELF IN

As my wife remarked on the way back, 'Don't you think privacy is overrated now? We got to know a very important local family and have had a very splendid time.'

So yes, I do think privacy can be overrated. If you enforce it, you build a wall between yourself and the world around you. You create antagonism, maybe suspicion or jealousy. In other words: the costs outweigh the benefits.

22

THE ORIGINS OF BOXING DAY

MANY YEARS AGO, our Christmas festivities had to be totally reorganised. Our twelve-year-old son was head chorister in a cathedral choir and Christmas Day for him was already fully booked with church services. So we decided to devote that day solely to religious observation and make Boxing Day the time for family and presents.

And so it was. First a day of endless Christmas carols, redeemed by the fact that it was our little boy who was singing them. And then we left for our home in Norfolk, with the car full of presents and the rest of the family.

And when we got there, everyone piled into the kitchen, ovens were turned on, food was prepared, presents were stacked under the tree and the Christmas festivities began.

In the end, we reckoned it was successful. We were not distracted from the religious side of things by

THE ORIGINS OF BOXING DAY

thoughts of the meal awaiting us. Duty done, we could celebrate without any feeling of guilt.

But it wasn't quite as good as in the distant days, when I was a little boy at home, in the Rectory in Ireland. Boxing Day back then was when we took cardboard boxes of food, vegetables, chocolates and oranges, provided by rich farmers, to slum parishes in Dublin.

I would be told to carry a box up to the front door, ring the bell and then, in a very embarrassed way, I would hand it over. I think it was much appreciated, though it was always just taken with a nod and an, 'Oh, thanks.' But we felt good about it anyway.

Originally Boxing Day in Britain was when church collection boxes, to which people had contributed during the year, were opened and the money they contained distributed to the poor of the parish. Our Irish version followed the same principle, though, of course, with food rather than cash.

I wonder if we shouldn't rethink our priorities – Christmas Day for religion, Boxing Day for boxes or money for the poor, and a celebration meal for ourselves. Then we could all feel well fed and virtuous at the same time.

PART 3
WORKING LIFE

23

TWO TYPES OF FREEDOM

I KNOW EXACTLY when it hit me. I was in my rather beautiful plantation-style house in South Malaya near Malacca, a lovely little town, playing bridge with my friends who were in the Army out there when I suddenly thought, 'This is not what I want to be doing with my life.'

At the time, I was the local Shell manager but all that really involved was keeping friendly with my main customers, the heads of rubber plantations or government departments. This meant asking them to endless dinner parties or luncheons on the beach, which was all very pleasant.

Shell was a benevolent employer. They guaranteed me a job for the rest of my life in various delectable parts of the world, with a generous salary which would continue after I retired in the form of a pension scheme.

I was trapped in a sort of comfortable prison. Then

I remembered Isaiah Berlin. This rather wonderful, but slightly secretive, professor at Oxford didn't teach much or write many books. But every so often he would emerge and focus what he called his 'intellectual spectacles' on some aspect of humanity which he would write up in a short essay. These often radically changed the way I thought about things.

One that particularly affected me was his essay on the two freedoms, the 'freedom from' and the 'freedom to'. At that moment, in my comfort zone in Malaya, I was enjoying 'freedom from': freedom from fear; freedom from poverty; freedom from worry; freedom from anything bad that might happen to me. Shell would look after me, I knew.

The trouble was, I had very little 'freedom to'.

I was supposed to be in charge of my branch of Shell, but everything was controlled. I could suggest things, but I couldn't decide anything on my own. Shell was run by endless rules and protocols and my team in Malacca were perfectly competent to do everything without me.

My job was to keep pouring wine down my main customers' throats, which was not what I thought my life was meant to be about. So, I had freedom from worry but no 'freedom to'. I was a sort of voluntary prisoner.

I resigned later that year and returned to England. I remember sitting with my wife on our first evening back

TWO TYPES OF FREEDOM

home. She produced a bottle of champagne to celebrate my 'real freedom' as she called it.

I said to her, 'But I'm only qualified to teach Latin to young boys at a prep school, which I don't want to do, and anyway they would only pay me enough to feed our dog, not ourselves.'

She said, 'I always hoped I would marry a professor who writes books, so why don't you do that?'

I answered, 'Well, I can try to do that but I don't see how I can be a professor of something that I've never studied – and anyway, where's the money going to come from?'

She said, 'We don't need much,' and I responded, 'Well, at the very least we need enough to feed the dog.'

In the end she found me a job teaching at the London Business School and I did write a book, and then many books, but it took a long time and I often wondered about my life at Shell. Why couldn't I be content with sitting in the sun, giving dinner parties, playing golf, reading books and drinking wine with my friends?

For some reason 'freedom from' wasn't enough for me. When I try to explain this to my teenage grandchildren as we talk about their future prospects, I tell them: it's very tempting to opt for 'freedom from' by pursuing a career that offers a fair guarantee of work and money for the rest of your working life. But then, like me, you will feel frustrated because really, secretly, you will want the 'freedom to' – the freedom to do what suits you better. That choice might involve less money than you'd like, and you won't be able to buy your children the education you'd like to or live in the type of house your partner might enjoy. But on the other hand, you will be satisfied by doing something that you really believe in, whatever that is.

Professor Berlin's point was that you can't have both, you have to choose. You will be pressurised to choose 'freedom from' but you may end up feeling frustrated. On the other hand, if you choose 'freedom to' you may be resigning yourself to a life of poverty.

So I pass the professor's dichotomy on to you and regret that I cannot offer a solution.

24

FEES OR WAGES?

THERE ARE TWO ways of paying people to work for you. You can either pay a wage which buys their time and you tell them what to do with that time. Or you pay them a fee which is for work done and delivered.

Now, I pay my cleaning lady a wage. When she arrives, I tell her what I'd like her to do. Much of the time is, in fact, spent having coffee with her. It is my privilege to spend her time like that and, I hope, her pleasure.

On the other hand, there's my lawyer. He rang me up in the morning to discuss my will and then he said, 'I am sending you a bill because I spent half of yesterday researching whether what you wanted for your dog was legal.'

'No,' I responded. 'I will pay you for my will when it is delivered. When and how you do your research is up to you. I am having a window made for my study – I don't want the builder to send me a bill halfway through for the time he spent measuring it up. That is part of what he has got to include in his calculations for his final bill. It's the same with you. When the will is delivered to my satisfaction, I will pay your fee.'

He didn't understand, but I insisted.

In this post-pandemic world, more people are working from home without supervision, so you can't check what they are doing or, indeed, whether they are doing anything. That is part of the delight of this new way of working – individuals are free to work when they want to. They can work in the middle of the night or in the early morning, or, like me, they can lie on the sofa, thinking.

But you still have to specify – and they have to agree – what the work is and when it is delivered. They will send you an invoice which may include their time spent, but that is up to them. Or they can charge nothing for their time spent and an awful lot for their wisdom and expertise.

As an artist explained when he was accused in a court of law of exploiting his client by charging her £500 an hour to paint her portrait: 'It's five hundred pounds per hour, but that includes a lifetime of experience and experiment.'

It's the same with me when I charge my clients a fee. They are buying my so-called wisdom, accumulated over many mistakes.

FEES OR WAGES?

So, when painters come to paint your house, you will pay them a fee when the work is done but that means you have no right to complain if you find them calling their mates on the phone out in the garden when you think they should be painting. If you want them working all the time, you have to pay them a wage and then you will have to supervise them and check their comings and goings – which is an awful waste of time.

The great delight of working from home is the freedom to do what you like, when you like. You build it all into the calculation of your fee, and everybody's happy.

So, work out whether you are paying your painter a fee or a wage. If you are paying a wage then it is your responsibility to supervise the work. If you pay a fee, then you just don't pay it if you don't like the finished result.

Fees or wages, make up your mind.

25

THE JOYS OF SELF-EMPLOYMENT

RECENTLY, UNEMPLOYMENT NUMBERS have been rising again. It reminds me of the time they last did so on this scale, some forty years ago. I had just published a book called *The Future of Work*. The BBC was planning a radio report on the same subject. So they sent a much younger Andrew Marr to interview me.

In the book, I'd argued there weren't enough jobs for the people who wanted them, but there was still an awful lot of work to be done in the world. We should go hunt it out for ourselves and create our own little businesses. It was already happening, I pointed out. I thought that within twenty years, the number of self-employed would more than balance the number of unemployed. Problem solved.

Andrew listened intently but looked more and more disbelieving as I went on. He concluded the interview by saying, 'Well, that was Charles Handy who believes that the number of self-employed will more than outnumber the unemployed. But as we talked, I looked out of the window and I saw a flock of pigs flying by.'

In other words, what I was saying was fantasy.

At the time I reckoned he was probably right. I thought back to how lucky I had been to have had a secure job with Shell International. I remembered then that when I met the Shell interview panel, they were noticeably unimpressed by my degree (which to them meant I had a well-organised mind, but an empty one which needed to be filled with something useful like chemistry or the nuts and bolts of running a business). But they perked up when I told them what I'd been doing in the holidays.

I had started a small-scale printing business in my bedroom at home using a second-hand Adana printing machine and two trays of metal type. I produced printed letterheads and invitation cards for the parents of my university friends. It was a nice little business which didn't make me rich but certainly made my time at Oxford much more enjoyable and boozy. I could see Shell thinking, 'Ah-ha, here's an entrepreneur in the making, we need more like that.' And they smiled encouragingly and offered me a job in their Singapore office which is where I went a year later.

But, of course, I was not allowed to be an entrepreneur out there.

After two well-paid years, but being just part of another big bureaucracy, I found myself missing the freedom I used to have running my own show. So I left Shell to try the academic life as a professor and worked for various Church of England organisations for four years.

I had assumed these benevolent bodies would allow me the freedom to be more innovative but I discovered to my dismay that they were as entangled in bureaucracy as Shell had been, and were staffed by people whose job in life seemed to be to stop me from doing any lateral thinking.

So, encouraged by my wife, I decided to practise what I preached: I gave up my salary and free house and became a freelance writer and speaker.

Now, there is no more insecure a career than that of a freelance actor or writer, and I struggled for a while. But in the end I loved it and I earnt much more, actually, than Shell had ever paid me.

So I encourage everybody to try a spell of flying solo. I can tell you, it's not as cold outside as it looks, once you get going. But if you're over forty, I suggest you pay off the mortgage before you take flight. Just in case.

THE JOYS OF SELF-EMPLOYMENT

I think that's what's going to happen again now – more and more people will go self-employed and find that it's fun. You don't have to have a boss. I urge you to try it.

26

GOODBYE NINE-TO-FIVE; HELLO OXFORD HOURS

THESE DAYS, MORE and more people are getting used to working at home in what I call 'sabbatical' time. So much so that they may well not want to go back to the old kinds of business hours.

In fact, I have long worked what I used to call 'Oxford hours', but which more truthfully are 'Army hours'.

It came about when I was still working a sort of office job at the London Business School. My wife asked me to come home one day for lunch with her father, a retired colonel, who was, to me, a slightly intimidating figure. So I said, 'Of course,' being an obedient husband in those days.

I came home at about half-past twelve and at two o'clock I began to excuse myself. I stood up and said, 'I am terribly sorry, but I have got to go back to the office.' The colonel looked at me from under his eyebrows.

GOODBYE NINE-TO-FIVE; HELLO OXFORD HOURS

'Good God, man,' he said. 'You don't mean to tell me you work in the afternoon?'

He went on to explain that in the Army, they got up early, they did their Army drills or whatever they were going to do in the morning, they had a couple of pink gins at lunchtime and in the afternoon rode ponies or did physical exercise of one sort or another and played sport. In the evening they socialised in the mess. He said that it made for a very balanced life. So I adopted it; I worked in the morning, I had a mild drink at lunch and I took exercise in the afternoon (though nowadays it is mostly just a walk around the garden). And I socialise in the evening, though not as heartily as I used to do.

I found this system worked very well. As someone without Army experience, I called it keeping 'Oxford hours', because basically that is what one tended to do in the university – work in the morning, physical exercise in the afternoon, socialise in the evening, sleep eventually, back to work in the morning.

It makes very good sense for a balanced life and I commend it to you, even without my father-in-law around to make sure I've earmarked enough time to look after his daughter.

27

RETHINKING THE WORKING WEEK

I WAS GETTING increasingly frustrated by the way my life was organised around me. You know, a working week of five days, a weekend of two days and an annual holiday of fifteen: how was I to live in this funny kind of truncated world where the working week was too long and the weekends too short? Then I started doing some mental arithmetic. I calculated that, according to my contract, I was allowed, if you added all these things and bank holidays together, over one hundred days of personal time a year, fully paid for, and divided up as I said, into weekends, weekdays and holidays.

So I said I'd like to have one day off work a week, which normally for me would be Monday but could change, banking the unused weekly day off. That way I'd build up enough holiday time to take ten-day breaks, to travel abroad to another city for fun and frivolity, to restore my spirits. When I started to put this new system into effect – I called it 'chunking' – I felt liberated; I was in charge of my own time, my most precious resource. Of course, I then had to fill the non-leisure days with useful work, but as Aristotle always said, you're happiest when you're at your best, working for the good of others, and that was entirely what I intended to do in one way or another. So, control of my time and happiness at hand.

Now, why don't more of us do that? Why do we accept the ways that society seems to have divided up our lives between work and pleasure? Why can't we decide to do things the way we like, not the way society likes?

Yes, I'm all for chunking – in time and in other ways too. I chunk my time between meditation and writing in the country, and socialising and celebrating culture in the capital. My wife and I used to chunk our domestic duties too – I was in charge of housekeeping and cooking when we were in the country, that was my chunk; my wife was in charge of it in London, that was her chunk. And we happily competed to create culinary delights.

So chunk as you please, my friends. Life is yours – make sure you control it.

28

IS KINDNESS AN ASSET IN BUSINESS?

IS KINDNESS a virtue or a weakness? I was brought up – as a son of the Rectory in the Irish countryside – to be kind to those worse off than me. If the doorbell rang, my father said, 'Always open it – it might be someone in need whom you can help.' I like that approach and believe in it.

A friend of mine, Gay Haskins, recently published a book called *Kindness in Leadership*, because she believes it's notably lacking.

Mind you, combining kindness and leadership is not as easy as you might think. As I found out for myself.

In my first command at Shell, I went out of my way to be kind and nice to all of my little team in Borneo where I ran the local subsidiary. My superiors back in Singapore were not impressed. They compared me to the mythical Chinese general who supposedly said to his troops, 'I'm your leader and I'm right behind you.'

IS KINDNESS AN ASSET IN BUSINESS?

'You put too much trust in your intelligence,' said my superiors, 'but you can't lead by starting on the back foot, let alone from the back room. You've got to be out in front, giving an example of what you want them to be. It's character, not intelligence, that makes a difference.'

Well, I obviously failed because they sent me back to London after two years and I devoted myself to writing about those people who did combine kindness with leadership, as well as those who should. Much more comfortable to be sitting in an armchair than walking off my back foot. Had this been now, of course, I would have pointed to Joe Biden, who seemed to do pretty well as a politician while being kind. 'Nice but dull,' my American friends would say of him. And, lucky man, the less he did and the less he said, the more everybody seemed to warm to him. Kindness was – and is – his basic ID.

I empathise strongly with Gay's views on the need for kindness, and it would be nice if being kind also proved to be conducive to better returns in business. Unfortunately the evidence doesn't always support my hope on that front, not at least if the two great maestros of American management in recent years – Jack Welch, the boss of General Electric, and Steve Jobs of Apple – are anything to go by.

General Electric under Welch was America's biggest and most profitable manufacturing business. Welch was known as Neutron Jack for his ability to get rid of swathes of people without in any way damaging the infrastructure of the business. He was also fond of his ten per cent rule – in any unit, he liked to reward or promote the top ten per cent and fire the bottom ten. It keeps them on their toes, he said. But keeping people on their toes for a long period of time is not nice and not kind. There was some compensation: those who were fired were quickly picked up by competitors, who hoped that some of Neutron Jack's ways had rubbed off on them.

And then there was Steve Jobs, who was notoriously difficult to work with; cruel and bullying to anyone who disagreed with him, but also a genius. His imagination, his ideas, and ultimately his products have, as he promised, changed the lives and work of almost every individual on the planet. People tell me it was very exciting to work at Apple, provided you didn't get too close to the man himself. But in my experience, 'exciting' is not an easy or fun way to live.

My Shell superiors wanted me to behave like a lieutenant in the First World War, leading my men out of the trenches under a hail of enemy fire, with a little wooden stick under my arm as a symbol of my authority while

IS KINDNESS AN ASSET IN BUSINESS?

they followed me into certain death. If that's kindness, it's not my sort of kindness, thank you very much.

So where does that leave us? Well, you are what you are. Some successful leaders treat others well; some don't. I am by nature kind to people; it's the way I was brought up, as I have already pointed out. Help a man up when he's down, I say. Give him a piece of bread and send him on his way. And help him to have high aspirations and to do his best with what he's got.

And run your organisation for the benefit of others, not for yourself. That's the main message, I think. Do as you would be done by, treat people fairly. Work for those less well off than yourself.

Teach your children to be generous to those who are less fortunate and not to be jealous of those who are better off.

In general, in an organisation, I'd rather be kind than a martinet – particularly if being a martinet means leading your troops to suicide.

29

THE POWER OF THE HUMBLE

AN ITEM I came across in *The Economist* reminded me how even the lowliest of us has more power than we think. It described how a householder in Essex managed to halt planning permission for a wind farm off the Essex coast.

It had been stopped because, he said, his complaint about the effect it would have on his view hadn't been taken into account in the assessment made by the government.

So one householder can stop planning permission for a huge wind farm. This is a reminder that even the meanest of us has the power to throw a spanner in the works. The receptionist, when you arrive at an organisation, can fail to connect you to the person you've come to see. The bus driver can refuse to open the doors on a rainy day to let you in because he or she is just feeling pissed off.

I've done it myself, sitting in the head office of Shell,

THE POWER OF THE HUMBLE

in the department grandly called Regional Marketing Europe. I was supposed to forward all documents from various European companies to the right department. I was just a post office worker really, but it sounded grand.

I discovered I did have a lot of power, though, because when an Italian company sent in a request to build a refinery on the edge of Pompeii, in the Bay of Naples, I was so outraged at the thought of such a wonderful historical site being dwarfed by a large industrial complex that I took action. It wasn't in my power to approve or refuse the application. I was just supposed to forward it to the board for their approval, but I realised I could do something else, and I did. I tore their ten-page proposal into little pieces and threw them in the waste bin.

All right, it's true that the chairman of the Italian company rang Shell's board of directors directly and they got their refinery. However, I'd managed to save Pompeii and the beautiful Bay of Naples from the corroding effects of a refinery on its shores for about three months, and I took that sense of power away with me when I went back home in the evening. I'd made a difference. A positive one.

But what about when it's a negative one? Anyone can throw a spanner in the works, no matter how low they are in the hierarchy. Sometimes people do it because they're fed up with the world, or because someone has been rude to them, or just because they've got a headache or the weather is depressing.

The only way to deal with the possibility of people in an organisation wielding negative power is to make sure everybody has a positive ability to make a difference, not a negative one. Allow them the freedom to make a positive contribution, otherwise they'll make a negative one because that's easier.

So think: what is the source of negative power in your organisation and what would it take for you to be enabled not to use it? To feel you had positive power rather than negative power? What about all your employees – have they got positive power or negative power? Think about it.

30

MY GRANDSON AND THE MARINES

I REMEMBER ALL too well the agonies of watching my little grandson trying to learn to ride his bike. Always falling off – luckily onto the grass – then picking himself up and trying again.

Eventually he said, 'Gaga, please go away, you're putting me off. I want to do this by myself.'

And I said to him, 'You're absolutely right. Make your mistakes in private; boast about your successes in public.'

In a funny way it made me think about how the US Marines operate. After every training project they have a follow-up session which involves certain rules. One is confidentiality – what's said in this room stays in this room, and any leaks will be heavily punished. Two: there should be no record of what's being said. These first two rules are there to encourage openness and honesty.

Then there's rule number three: no blame or

reprimand is to be extended for mistakes made on the training project, even in jest by your colleagues.

So they all sit down and admit their mistakes. And nobody blames them. Discussions are had and everyone learns by the things they've done wrong. And in their personnel files there are no horrendous blunders documented, only records of achievement.

When I joined Shell oil company, they didn't believe in training sessions. They dumped you right in at the deep end, giving you your own independent command at the age of thirty in some far-away country where no one would notice if you did something wrong, and where no one from HQ would visit you until you'd been there at least ten years – which meant you had a lot of time not only to correct your mistakes, but to achieve some successes to show off to your bosses. That's what happened to me.

Shell's approach wasn't the same as that of the Marines but luckily it ended up with the same result for me. It meant there were no blotches in my files detailing the horrible mistakes I made – just the records of my wonderful performance in boosting sales for the company.

It amazes me that more organisations don't do the same as the Marines. Too often people don't admit the mistakes they've made because they're afraid of being reprimanded or dealt with harshly in some way. Sometimes they blame the mistake on somebody else or find some other excuse to cover their tracks. It can all get very messy.

But if they were working in an environment where they felt happy to admit the mistakes they made, they'd be in a position to discuss how things went wrong, listen to the views of others and learn from their mistakes . . . and eventually find some successes to boast about in public.

Just like my grandson did.

Good luck with all your mistakes.

31

THE IMPORTANCE OF LEAVING WELL ALONE

IT'S A LONG, LATIN-BASED word but very important: subsidiarity. Try saying it, remembering it and spelling it. You could say it's a long word for a short idea – delegation. But it's much more important than that. It's part of Catholic social teaching and it says: it is immoral – against moral order – for a higher authority to take decisions that properly could be taken by a lower-order body, closer to the action.

So, for instance, the government shouldn't tell teachers how to teach young kids to read – that's the job of the teachers; and if they can't do it, then they should be trained to do it, but the government shouldn't interfere with the teacher's job.

In the later stages of the Covid pandemic, the UK government practised subsidiarity when it told people to make their own decision whether or not to wear face masks in public, and whether to meet people inside as

THE IMPORTANCE OF LEAVING WELL ALONE

well as outside. Quite right too, though I suspect they didn't know it was a moral decision. It's very important that we shouldn't steal people's choices from them.

I remember so well being allowed to walk home from school when I was, I think, ten. It was under half a mile on country roads in Ireland. I was secretly aware that my dad was following me on his bicycle, but all the same, I made it on my own, and there was a special cake for tea.

When it came to my own kids in London, my wife and I allowed them to take the bus, but we took the precaution of tying a label around them with our address and telephone number on it. And when they returned home, safely and on time, there was more special cake for tea because they'd made their own decision and taken responsibility.

And so it went on. As they grew up and started having romantic liaisons, we had to be very careful not to interfere with their decisions and choices, much though we wanted to.

Then when they began having children, we often wanted to tell them how to behave with their offspring but had to restrain ourselves, remembering that it's immoral to steal people's responsibilities or choices.

It would be a much more exciting world if everybody was allowed to get on with their own business, take their own decisions. It would be a lively world – and a lively family – if everybody did their own thing.

Of course, people in the centre want to control everything, but they should be told it's immoral to steal people's choices, their decisions. Making choices is an important part of growing up and developing. Of course, ask for advice if you want it – but make the final decision your responsibility. This is the best way to run a business, the best way to run a family, the best way to run a household.

My wife and I had a rule: never give advice to our children unless they ask for it. Of course, sometimes I'd find myself saying to them, 'If you were to ask my advice, I would tell you . . .' Then my wife would look at me and I would shut up.

It's true that sometimes people like to be told what to do. Like at first with Covid, many people wanted guidelines from the government. But there comes a time we have to take responsibility. I believe it's as much of a sin not to live up to your responsibilities as it is to deny them.

So practise subsidiarity in your life, your family and your work. You'll be surprised at how exciting they all become.

32

MY FANTASY OFFICE

IN RECENT YEARS, we have tried turning the home into the office, and for some of us it has worked well. Now I think it is perhaps the right moment to try and turn the office into the home – but one with the home's drudgeries and distractions.

What do I mean by the drudgeries of home? Well, first of all, the persistence at home of cleaning everything before and after use. My wife used to delight in the polished sheen of a mahogany dining table, but for me, now that I am responsible for creating that sheen, every smudge is a signal of drudgery to come. The distractions for me mostly come in the form of small children and pets.

So can I have the companionship that I treasure and the comforts that I love without all these drudgeries and distractions? How did my ancestors manage it? Well, of course, they created the gentlemen's club, many examples of which now line the streets of Pall Mall and St James's.

I distracted myself recently by designing my fantasy office. It won't look like the sort in colonial mansions of old; it'll be much more contemporary, probably located on the eastern side of London to acknowledge that's where the new intelligentsia are drifting. It will be more curvilinear than straight-lined, contemporary and sleek rather than traditional. A place of allure, however – somewhere you want to belong to, you want to go into.

Once in, there are staff everywhere, unlike at home. And what you notice first is that there are lots of rooms but that they are not allocated to specific people whose names are on the doors, but to activities. So there's a room for eating – very important. There is a library full of books but also large sofas and very comfortable armchairs smelling mustily of learning and offering an invitation, one might say, to somnolence as long as it is silent.

There are meeting rooms galore and private offices that you can book if you want to be alone. There is a very sophisticated tech office with every convenient sort of computer magic laid on and a technical assistant to show you how to access the various features. There is a presentation room for staff or clients to use whenever they wish. It's equipped with all the latest visual aid technology, of course. Everything here is the latest design.

MY FANTASY OFFICE

There are changing rooms and showers for weary commuters or sweat-stained cyclists. But the dominant feature is the food counter, which runs the length of the room and that reminds you more and more that this is not an office but something more like the first-class lounge at an airport terminal. There is comfortable seating everywhere, some workstations around the room, but mostly just coffee tables and this enormous food counter.

A hot breakfast is served for free, every morning, from nine o'clock on, encouraging an early start. And when you arrive, you pick up your cell phone from where it's been charging overnight in the entrance hall and promise never to turn it off, because that is your contact mechanism.

After you've had your breakfast, you can settle down to plan your day. Many will book an office, some will go out to meet clients or contractors or planners or architects or whatever. Others will go home. Everyone will spend at least one half-day a week working from home, still with their cell phone on, of course.

At the food counter, alcohol has to be paid for or signed for. In the evening, the place resembles a sort of supper club, with great camaraderie.

It is a sociable place. One of the senior partners sits

in a glass-walled room at the end of the lounge, popping out occasionally to have a cup of coffee or an informal talk with a colleague who has wandered past or has signalled they'd like a chat. It is all very smart-casual but also sleek and efficient.

So how much time do people spend in this office? Well, the informal rule is that all meetings should be on Wednesdays and Thursdays, if possible, so they tend to be in for the middle of the week. But it is such a pleasant place to be and so easy to work in that it draws people at all times, particularly early in the morning and in the evening.

Though I don't expect long-established organisations to turn themselves into business-class lounges, I do think the elements of the old-fashioned club culture will start to creep into the corporate world as people seek some of the comforts of home without the drudgeries and distractions of it. They want a workplace that is a pleasure and a delight to spend time in, and a work culture that still allows you to creep off home – if that's where you work best. The signs are that we may well be drifting to a world of working from home with some office meetings – and left largely to ourselves to decide what the mixture will be.

To me this seems ideal. I don't like to be a human resource or to be told when or how to work. I like

MY FANTASY OFFICE

the camaraderie of the office. I also like the pleasures of being alone at home. If I can manage to have both then I am well pleased. Whether my fantasy office ever becomes a reality, we shall see.

33

GROW BETTER, NOT BIGGER

I WAS STANDING in a lovely little winery in the middle of the Napa Valley in California. The owner was very friendly and we got chatting.

Looking around me down the valley, all I could see were rows and rows of vines, everywhere, square miles of them.

'Goodness,' I said to him, 'the whole valley is a vineyard.'

'Yes,' he said, 'they're all my competitors, damn them. But I'm going to beat them.'

'How?' I asked. 'I don't see any spare land around here – are you going to buy them out?'

'No,' he replied. 'I'm going to grow better, not bigger. If I can come in the top two or three in the annual tastings this year, I can wipe the floor with them – that'll teach 'em.'

'Hmm,' I thought, 'better not bigger – that's interesting.'

GROW BETTER, NOT BIGGER

Later on that day I was talking to the head of a family business. He said he wanted the family to be immortal. Their name was on the product they made, and by making the business more and more successful in the future, they too would, in a way, last forever.

'Well, in that case,' I replied, 'you ought to make sure that your aim every year is to be better, not bigger. There's no way you can make enough product to cater for the whole market. Immortality is the ultimate challenge – you have to keep reinventing yourself, bringing in new talent, raising your standards. Only that way will the family firm last.'

And then I decided to look at myself, a writer. Of course I'd love to come up with a bestselling novel, perhaps a raunchy political thriller, but I don't have the imagination for that. I write about organisations and the people in them.

I said to myself: why don't I listen to my own advice? If I try to be better at what I do, maybe I can earn more money than my rivals.

So I applied myself to making my books a little more interesting – even though the subject was necessarily a bit dull.

And I got my reward with the first review of my next book. It read something like, 'There's nothing in this book that hasn't been said before . . .' (my heart sank)

'. . . but the point is, it will never have been *read* before until you pick up this fascinating book.'

And so it worked.

That book has now sold many hundreds of thousands of copies – far outselling any raunchy novels by my rivals and giving me many opportunities to speak to thousands of business executives around the world (even if they may have been bored out of their minds).

So think 'better' not 'bigger' – in your organisation and in whatever you want to achieve. It's less exhausting, more exciting, and, in the end, more profitable, as my friend in Napa Valley knew well.

34

MY NEW BUSINESS IDEA

DO ORGANISATIONS HAVE memories? Of course they do – though sometimes these can be a bit faulty.

For a number of years, I was chairman of the Royal Society of Arts, a prestigious British institution, located in a lovely building just off the Strand in London.

Recently, I went back there to listen to a lecture.

When I entered, the receptionist, a very nice young woman, asked to see my membership card.

I said, 'I don't need one,' and pointed to the panels above her head, which listed all the chairmen from the past 100 years. I said, 'My name is up there: Charles Handy, Chairman, 1987 to 1989.'

She said, 'Oh, yes,' in an uninterested tone. 'So can I see your membership card?'

Luckily a member of staff passed by just then and was able to assure her I was indeed a fellow and entitled to enter.

The receptionist was unimpressed.

I suppose she was within her rights to stop me, but I couldn't help feeling very annoyed as I left the building. After years of hard work at the Society – and in my opinion having, in a sense, rescued the organisation from ruin – to be forgotten was quite hurtful.

But then sometimes memories can be annoying.

When I worked for Shell in Singapore, one of my colleagues had spent fifteen years in West Africa. And at every meeting, every time I came up with a great idea, he would say, 'Oh, we tried that in Ghana . . . or was it Nigeria? . . . and it never worked.' And I would curse his damned memory.

But of course it wasn't *his* memory, I later realised – so much as the collective memory of the Shell group of companies of which there were some 250.

And then I thought, 'Hmm, why doesn't Shell harvest all these memories and record and catalogue them? So if someone comes across a difficult situation or problem, they can input a description of it and see who else has had the same issue and learn from their experience.'

Because that's how you learn. I've always said that learning is experience understood upon reflection. It helps if it's your experience, but other people's experiences are almost as good. And Shell had a whole load of other people's experiences to draw upon.

MY NEW BUSINESS IDEA

In fact, if you could harvest and catalogue them (along with, perhaps, the experiences of other organisations), you'd have a very valuable collection of what you might call case studies.

Indeed – and here's where this becomes a business thought – one could license them, so that people would pay a subscription to gain access to this library of experiences. Or you could publish the material as a book, a scholarly study or some kind of anthology.

Now there's a thought.

I'm too lazy to do anything about this idea but if any of you wants to start a new business based around the idea of a library of experiences, please feel free to go ahead. I would like some acknowledgement somewhere, and perhaps an invitation to the launch party if you have one.

Such a memory bank of experiences could also be used in a teaching setting, and at the end of the class one could even invite the original people who sent in their memories to come and tell everybody how it all worked out. Students always love to meet the real actors, I find.

And the idea of the collective memory applies to family life too. Going through my photo albums, I couldn't remember who half of the faces were. But someone else in the family always could . . .

'Oh, yes, that's Julian's uncle,' they would say. 'Oh,

that's your grandmother trying to have a pee by the roadside after our picnic.'

And so it went on, bringing up memories from the past, sharing them with the family. A library of family experiences can be very worthwhile.

Once again, if you like my business idea, please go ahead, I'd love to see somebody do it.

PART 4
EVERYDAY LIFE

35

THE POWER OF NAMES

MANY YEARS AGO now, I was sitting on our terrace in the apartment we owned in Tuscany, when I looked at the scrappy little patch of grass covering the ground below.

I thought how nice it would be to turn it into a decent lawn. I went back to England, photographed our lawn in Norfolk, brought the picture back, showed it to Dino, our Italian gardener, and said, 'Dino, I'd like the lawn to look like this.'

When we came back later that summer, I was horrified to find the lawn covered in weeds: daisies and dandelions.

I said to Dino, 'What happened? Why didn't you cut it like I showed you?'

He said, 'Oh, but that would have destroyed all the lovely flowers.'

'What flowers?' I asked. He pointed and I looked at the lawn through his eyes and saw, yes, he was right: the dandelions and daisies looked lovely against the background of dark green grass. They weren't weeds; they were flowers.

So, I left it alone and in future I would invite my visitors to come and sit on what I christened my 'lawn of flowers'.

They thought it was delightful. I thought, 'Well, well, well: just call something a different name and you see it differently.'

When we were in lockdown, as it was called, I thought of it to myself as an overdue sabbatical. This is the word academics use for holidays in which they do some serious catching up in their particular field of study, which in my own institution came every seven years.

According to *Leviticus* 25, Jews in the Land of Israel must take a year-long break from working the fields every seven years. So when my friends rang me up during lockdown and asked how I was doing, I would say, 'I am enjoying my sabbatical very much.' 'Lucky you,' they would say. 'We are in lockdown, and it's hell.' 'Ah,' I would reply, 'well, just name it differently and you might think of it differently. Call it your honeymoon.'

They thought I was joking of course. But I was being serious.

There are other examples. I wondered what would

THE POWER OF NAMES

happen if we called income tax 'a donation to the nation's wellbeing' rather than tax. Might we feel better about it?

I talked to my accountant and said, 'If I were to go on to the Just Giving website, and if there were a fund called Donations to the National Wellbeing and I donated the equivalent of a month's tax on a regular basis, would that be good, do you think?'

He said, 'Not only good, it would be very beneficial because it would count as a donation and be tax-deductible, so it would reduce your final bill.'

So I thought, 'If I start doing that, not only will I feel good about donating to the country's future wellbeing, but also, when I get the final tax assessment, I will look at it with joy because it will be so little.'

Maybe I should suggest this to the government. But, in future, I am going to refer to the tax I pay as my voluntary donation – and see if just calling it that will make a difference to the way I feel about it.

Think about it.

36

THE RISE OF EMPATHY

I WOKE UP one morning during the Covid pandemic to a brilliant sunshiny day and remembered Robert Browning's lines, 'Oh, to be in England / Now that May is there'. (Yes, I know he said 'April', but I thought I'd put May just to keep you on your toes.) It really was lovely and I thought I'd be brave and go downtown. Where I live, that means going to Putney High Street. Not the most vibrant centre in the world, but very full of traffic, as always, and, on that day, inevitably, not many people.

However, I needed to cross the road to get to the bank.

I was still a bit wobbly on my feet after my stroke. So I turned to a man beside me, a total stranger. I plucked up courage and I said, 'Would you mind helping me across the street?' He said, 'Sure, mate,' with a smile. He gave me his arm and, together, we stumbled across.

THE RISE OF EMPATHY

We hadn't been introduced but we didn't need to be. By the time we got to the other side I knew his name, his age, where he lived, his medical history and how he earnt his living. He knew the same about me. When I said I was an author and wrote about the future, he said, 'Oh, I can't be doing with that. I think the present is quite bad enough.' Anyway, we were bosom friends by the time we reached the bank. We said goodbye, and I thought to myself later as I watched the inevitable news coverage of Covid statistics, 'Well, it isn't all bad.'

It might just have been the sunshine but I felt there was a new mood descending, at least on Putney. A mood I can only describe as one of empathy, a genuine feeling that the world is full of kindness, that people are full of sympathy and ready to help. A world of generosity and hope where strangers are not rivals or enemies but potential friends.

The stranger I encountered sent me on my way with a feeling of real hope. My spirits were boosted. And I thought to myself: 'Well now, that's a title for my next book – *The Age of Empathy*.' Unfortunately, it has already been written. But I can heartily recommend it. Its full title is *The Age of Empathy: Nature's Lessons for a Kinder Society* and it is by Frans de Waal.

It seems there is altruism embedded in all of us. We

only need to make it fashionable to let it out. It would be nice to think that the pandemic sparked in us a desire for a new age of empathy, a mood of mutual understanding and support, of helpfulness and hope.

37

WHY OWNERSHIP IS A TRAP

A BIG EVENT in my grandchildren's lives was the arrival of a new puppy, Ziggy, of indeterminate parentage but very sweet. Inevitably, it sparked a competition among them as to who could cuddle it next.

I said, 'Be careful as you rush around it. You are falling into the ownership trap.'

'What's that?' asked Scarlett, the youngest.

'It's when you think you own something but it turns out that it owns you. See, look at you now. You are rushing around looking after this puppy. You thought you owned it so you could do with it what you want. But actually you have to look after it – ownership brings responsibilities. You have to feed it, exercise it, train it, keep it well, make sure it has the right food and the right medicines as well as the right cuddles. Look at you, you are slaves to this puppy. It owns you.

'But worse, when you get older, you will think that you want to own a house. And then you are going to be slaves to a house. Slaves to a puppy is one thing; slaves to a house, that's crazy. When your granny and I first lived here, we rented it from Colin Anderson who owned the place. If the boiler went wrong, which it often did, I would ring him up and say, "Colin, the boiler's gone again," and he would say, "Oh, dear, I will get a plumber and if necessary we'll put a new boiler in." And I thought, "Well, that's solved that, and it hasn't cost me anything."

'But then I bought the house from him, quite cheaply because he was making no money out of it. And now I own it. So when I need a new boiler, as I did last week, I have to get the plumber in and pay for it myself. I have to paint the window frames, I have to check the drains, I have to repair the roof if it leaks. I am a slave to this house. That's crazy. Why should I be owned by a house when I thought I owned it? So watch out, don't own anything!

'Your generation seems to understand this. People these days share far more than my generation did, partly out of necessity, of course, but partly from preference. They share houses, they share the school run, they share dogs, they share holidays, they share holiday homes. And I quite understand the point. If you share it, you share the expenses and you share the responsibilities – you are all slaves together.

'But if you don't share, then you are working for the

house – which is crazy. Let somebody else look after it and I'll just rent, and then I can move if I want to. If I take a job in Oxford not London, I can go and rent something in Oxford. I am flexible. I think that's much better. And if I can do it by sharing then it doesn't cost me anything.

'This flat that I'm in, Flat One, has a lawn behind it, a beautiful big lawn, the size of two tennis courts. When I was renting it, I had to cut the grass, as nobody else did. So in the end I got the other six people who lived in the building to come together and I said, "Let's redefine the lawn as common space, which means you will own it as well as me. We will take it in turns to cut the grass."

'One of my neighbours said, "Well, no, I would rather that together we paid a part-time gardener to cut the grass." And so we went with that plan.

'The next Sunday we had our picnic on the lawn, newly cut by Tom, the part-time gardener. And I saw to my pleasure that there were six other picnics in progress. And that seemed to be quite right: we were all sharing the lawn. And now everybody was happy. It cost less, and we all shared it so we were all friends.

'So please don't own anything. Rent it or, if possible, share it – or give it away.'

38

PERSONALITY vs CHARACTER

CHARACTER OR PERSONALITY? Which do you think is more important? Some will argue: aren't they the same thing? But they're not. And there's the rub, as Shakespeare might say.

Character reveals itself over time once you are in the job. It's formed and shaped by your reactions to events and situations.

Personality, on the other hand, is the mask you put on before the rest of the world. To an extent it's something you can shape. And those who are able can achieve success in business and in politics. Think, for example, of those political leaders who started life as actors or entertainers and can 'play' people with big personalities. Think of Ronald Reagan in the USA and President Zelensky in Ukraine. (I think Sir Keir Starmer might usefully spend some time in a drama school, poor man.)

Personality, however, is no measure of character.

PERSONALITY VS CHARACTER

People sometimes used to tell me I didn't have the character to be a leader. But they were mistaking my personality for my character. In terms of personality, I'm a modest guy, thoughtful and very unassuming, timid even, and reserved in public. Certainly not a lively, charismatic type. Character-wise, on the other hand, I've demonstrated myself to be determined and resilient in my professional life.

Because there's this gap between personality and character, we often make wrong choices when it comes to appointing leaders. In businesses and in governments, we frequently choose someone whose personality we like, only to find that their character is weaker than we thought. And in some cases, even more corrupt than we thought. The man or woman we believed to be so thoughtful turns out to be egotistical, autocratic, unable to take advice, unable to listen, and temperamental.

Conversely, a candidate for leadership might have the character required for the job but not the personality needed to get themselves chosen. Which can be very bad news when it comes to elections, as we miss out on the leader we deserve.

It's a tricky game and it's sad to think that it affects our democracy so deeply.

All I can do is wish you luck in decoding the personality to find the character.

39

THE JOY OF TEACHING

I JUST HEARD this morning that a daughter of a friend of ours had given up her posh job in a big bank to do home schooling for her nephews and nieces. Lucky nephews and nieces, I say. Aunts and uncles are much more fun than parents and so make much better teachers – they listen whereas parents just preach all the time. Aunts and uncles were naughty once; parents never. Aunts and uncles are also acceptable as authority figures – they're meant to be wise and wonderful; parents are just annoying.

And my guess is that the aunts and uncles will enjoy the process just as much as the children will. I've recently noticed that my teenage grandson Leo is teaching my carer to play chess, and loving it. When I ask him to play chess with me, he doesn't seem to want to. Sometimes teachers have more fun than students. So, well, why don't we all become teachers?

If you're a good footballer, why not teach some local

kids your skills? You might find it wonderful fun. My great hero Aristotle said doing your best at what you're best at for the good of others is what makes you really happy in life. So if you're good at something, why not try teaching it to others?

When I became a teacher, I found I learnt much more than the students because I had to work out exactly why things worked the way they did, whether I was teaching history or geography or chemistry or whatever, while they just had to listen. I bet my grandson now knows far more about chess than he ever did before.

So, to anyone who's able to: on your bikes, save some kids from the tedium of home schooling – and feel good about it in the process. Or if you don't have young relatives in school, take some time this weekend to ponder what skill you could pass on to others. It'll make you feel happy. At least that's what I've found, and so did Aristotle nearly 2,500 years ago.

40

THE PAST WON'T HELP THE FUTURE

I AM CONSTANTLY bemused by the fuss made over exam results.

When I took my driving test, nobody was interested in my experience as a cyclist; they said it was a different experience. Quite right too. I had to take another series of tests to get a driving licence.

When I applied to study Classics at Oriel College, Oxford, they took no notice of my five distinctions at Higher Certificate level – what are now called A-levels. They said they weren't relevant. At Oxford they were going to teach me to think and they wanted to know how I would manage if I had to think on my own. How would I deal with a question like 'Why do we work?' for which any knowledge I had acquired so far would be totally irrelevant?

So I had to take their exam, which was very difficult. And once I had studied at Oxford and got my first-class

THE PAST WON'T HELP THE FUTURE

degree, of which I was very proud, I applied to Shell – who took no notice of it. They asked me to do their own business studies tests. And I understood why. When I took my first job with them, running their operations in Borneo, in East Asia, my knowledge of Greek and Latin was of no use at all whereas my experience of doing their case studies was relevant.

So, test on admission, not on exit, is my philosophy.

But there is a more important point here and that is: should the past be your guide to the future? I hope not, because if it were, nothing would ever change. Tomorrow would be like yesterday, next year like last year.

Of course there are people who wish it was that way; that everything remained the same or that, as one person put it to me, 'the status quo should be the way forward'. For my part, I think that's horrible.

When I wake up in the morning, I think with relief that it's a new day, a chance to reinvent myself, to be more imaginative, to be more adventurous, to be kinder, nicer, more interesting. Not the same old boring chap that I was yesterday. And the same with next year – next year will be better than last year because I shall be more interesting and I'll be more adventurous.

So, how well I did in one experience is no guide to how I'll do in the next. I hope I will do better. Because it will be different.

Therefore please don't rate people by how they did in the experience before last because it's irrelevant. Riding a bicycle gives you no clue how to drive a car.

And please remember: tomorrow is another opportunity to be different from the person you were yesterday.

41

LET'S DO AWAY WITH DICHOTOMIES

ANOTHER FAMILY MEETING this morning. 'Would we all like to go to the seaside? It's time for a little walk on the beach.' To which I replied, 'I can think of nothing worse than walking along a snowy beach by the North Sea in February. And,' I added, 'worse still, you'll be falling into the trap of a dichotomy.'

'What's that?' they asked.

'It's a logical error,' I said. 'A dichotomy is when you're faced with taking one of two alternatives – as in Brexit: in or out. Or as in most referenda: yes or no. And you've just given me one: North Sea or not – when in fact there are plenty of other choices.'

Dichotomies are often thought to be helpful because they simplify life. They're much loved by politicians because voters can very often be persuaded to select the choice those in power prefer. But in my view dichotomies are dangerously simplistic because they leave out other possibilities.

So you must always, when encountering dichotomies, add a few buts – such as: 'No, I don't want to go to the North Sea, but I can see it would be good for us to get out of this house so why don't we go to my favourite restaurant, if it's open?' Or, 'Why not sit by the fire and watch rugby and see other people running around in the cold?' Or, 'Yes, I'd love to walk along the beach, but shouldn't we wait for a warmer day, when the sun is shining and the wind has dropped?'

Without such buts, there's a danger that we reduce the world to a set of contradictory alternatives, and that stifles our imagination and leaves out all the other possibilities.

So what did the family do? We sat by the fire and watched the rugby.

Personally, I'd like to outlaw dichotomy as a device in political decision-making, on the grounds that it invariably over-simplifies and restricts our creativity.

I know parents sometimes use dichotomies when disciplining their children: 'Either you eat this or you go to bed.' The possibility that they might eat a little of it and then watch the telly is not mentioned. I

LET'S DO AWAY WITH DICHOTOMIES

think that it's very unfair indeed to limit their choices in this way.

So to parents, politicians and everyone else – avoid dichotomies like poison. And if you must use one, allow some buts or amendments.

42

WHY DIFFERENCES MAKE A DIFFERENCE

ON OUR WEDDING anniversary, after ten happy years of marriage, my wife and I decided to make a list of all the wonderful things we had in common. Much to our surprise, we found there weren't that many. She loved skiing, I found it terrifying; she loved sailing, I found it uncomfortable unless we were becalmed on a warm and sunny day; most importantly, when we took decisions, she relied on her gut instinct as she called it, while I relied on evidence and logic.

So our discussions were very argumentative. Unfortunately, I discovered that she was almost always right, even though she couldn't explain why. Early on in our marriage, we were visited by a man from Lloyd's of London who wanted to check that I understood what I was doing when I'd applied to be a Name: that I had pledged a significant amount of my assets, including my home, to back their insurance bets.

WHY DIFFERENCES MAKE A DIFFERENCE

'Don't trust that man,' my wife said when he left.

'Why not? I thought he was very competent.'

'He wears brown shoes on a weekday with a grey suit – not to be trusted.'

'Why not?' I asked.

She said, 'I can't explain it – that's your job.'

Well, it turned out she was right. Despite all this man's promises about the rewards I would reap, I ended up writing out cheques for tens of thousands of pounds for the next five years.

After that, I tried to work out why her gut instinct had been right. In this case it had told her that because the man wore the uniform of a weekend golfer, and not that of an insurance specialist, it was likely he didn't know what he was talking about.

As the years went by, we made a wonderful partnership: she with her gut instincts and me with my evidence and logic. Our differences made a big difference to our marriage.

Differences can also make a big difference in the workplace. Take Margaret Thatcher and Abraham Lincoln. When Thatcher formed a Cabinet, she wanted people who thought the same way she did – were 'one of us', as she put it. That meant she could be guaranteed a harmonious discussion. So much so, I was told, that she felt able to sum it up before it started and challenge anyone to disagree with her. Of course this led to tyranny, which always ends in disaster – in her case with her decision to introduce the unpopular Poll Tax that led to the end of her reign.

Lincoln, on the other hand, composed his Cabinet from what has been called a team of rivals – people who had opposed him in his run for the presidency or would have liked to. This meant he ended up with a wide range of competencies – and, of course, of opinions – which meant that better, more broad-based discussions could be had.

John Kennedy's two big decisions on Cuba are often cited as examples of why differences make a difference. On the first one, about the invasion of the Bay of Pigs, Kennedy relied on an advisory group made up mainly of the heads of the Services, who unanimously favoured an invasion and were confident it would succeed. It was of course a colossal failure.

The second time round, when Cuban missiles were about to be armed with nuclear warheads by the Russians, his brother Bobby suggested he widen the advisory group to include people other than the Service chiefs. This helped Kennedy to come up with a solution that persuaded the Russians to call back their ships and so avoid a nuclear war.

WHY DIFFERENCES MAKE A DIFFERENCE

The 'differences' in that advisory group made all the difference and averted a potential global catastrophe. Just by introducing a little difference. Not a bad outcome.

43

HAPPINESS, THE CHINESE WAY

I WOULD LIKE to remind you of the Chinese definition of happiness:

As Confucius says – to be happy you need something to work on, something to hope for and someone to love. Please note, you have to do the loving and only if you are lucky do you get something in return; it's not someone to love you, it's you to love someone.

The slog goes on because work, it seems, is essential to happiness. Work and other people, particularly the family – those closest to you.

At the moment I tick all three boxes – work, hope and lots of people to love, most of them under the age of sixteen. So, I am kept pretty busy.

I hope you can tick all three as well. Remembering that work is essential, that having other people to love is essential, and also to hope, even if it's for something a long way away.

44

THE NARCISSUS SYNDROME

IN MY TEENAGE years, my father, who was the local Rector, invited me to read the lesson at morning service. I must say, I quite enjoyed standing behind the lectern, ornamented with a big bronze eagle, reading aloud the wonderful words of the Authorised version of the Bible, rolling my tongue around the sentences.

That was until we went home for lunch and my mother said, 'You looked very pleased with yourself, young man, up at that lectern, holding forth from the Bible. I must say, it didn't look nice. I was not pleased. You'll soon have all the kids in the village mocking you. You remind me of that story you told me about the Greek boy who was in love with his own reflection.'

'Oh, yes,' I said, 'you mean Narcissus – he was so fascinated by his reflection on the water that he tried to get close to it, fell in and drowned.'

'Well,' my mother said, 'you'd better be careful.'

At least he gave his name to my favourite flower.

I didn't tell my mother then that he also gave his name to a devastating mental illness which goes by the name of NPD or narcissistic personality disorder. NPD appears to be incurable, mainly because the people who have it are so pleased with themselves, like Narcissus, they can't believe they suffer from any illness at all, so have no interest in finding a cure. They think they're perfect.

I call it the Emperor Syndrome; think Nero in Roman times or Putin today.

But it happens in ordinary life too. I've had bosses who suffered from Emperor Syndrome. When I was in Singapore with Shell, there was one who would come in each morning and say, 'Good morning, everybody,' at which we would all spring to attention and stand by our desks. He would then march down the lines between us, nodding to one or two people, very much as if he was royalty, and we had to respond politely.

One time, reaching me, he stopped and said, 'Everything OK, Charles?' And I replied, 'Yes, sir, thank you, sir,' and he moved on to his inner sanctum.

When he'd gone my neighbour Tony asked me what that was all about. I said I didn't know.

'Well, he stopped and spoke to you but he blanked me,' Tony said. 'That seems like a bad omen. I wonder what he's got in store for me.'

THE NARCISSUS SYNDROME

I said, 'I'm sure he just forgot your name for a moment and didn't want to stumble over it so he went on.' But Tony wasn't satisfied and sat there worrying for the rest of the morning.

Come the end of the day, we all stood to attention as the boss came by again to leave.

'Good afternoon,' he said, and we all replied, 'Good afternoon, sir,' and off he went.

Very high and mighty he was. Well, actually not very high – quite short really, so he looked like a puffed-up corporal rather than a general. Of course, he had no medals because he wasn't in the Army. The best he could do was his old school tie, which I didn't recognise.

The next day we heard he'd died from a heart attack – possibly brought on by the stress of keeping up the appearance of someone who was very important.

45

WHAT DOES 'FAIR' MEAN?

WE ALL BELIEVE in a just society, a fair society. But before you start changing the taxation system or the salary scale in your organisation, you need to work out what you mean by 'just society', and what you mean by 'fair'.

For instance, do you think it's fair that people should get what they deserve? That if they do their job well, they should be paid more, and if they do it badly, they should be paid less? If you do, you believe in meritocracy, a word that was first used by Michael Young, a social reformer.

Young, in spite of coining this word, did not believe in meritocracy. He said it created a bloc of self-satisfied people at the top of society who smugly thought they deserved all the good things they got, and that those at the bottom deserved all the bad things they got. People at the top were selfish and had no social conscience. Meritocracy leads, he said, to a divided society.

WHAT DOES 'FAIR' MEAN?

Or would you go with the Christian view: those who need most should get most, and those who have most should give most – that's only fair? I suppose politicians might call that levelling up, but levelling up in one area inevitably means that some have to level down.

Or do you believe, like me, that nobody should be either lavishly enriched or overly impoverished – that there should be a minimum which applies to everybody?

It's something to think about – not just regarding humanity at large, but on a family scale too. If you give pocket money to your children, for instance, do you give more to the eldest, or more to the child you think needs it more, or do you give an equal sum to each child? There is no easy right or wrong, it depends on your view of life. But ponder it before you start doing anything.

46

A THOUGHT ON RITUAL

LIKE ME, YOU may well have been enthralled by the endless ritual involved in the handing over of the monarchy from one generation to the next. I think ritual is terribly important: it emphasises continuity and change at the same time – things that are crucial within all organisations.

I often wonder why the Church of England hasn't devised a religious ceremony for divorcing couples. One which celebrates the good things and times gone by and asks for blessing and guidance for the two lives that are about to diverge.

I say this because I believe that continuity and change are vitally important in private lives as well as in public life. We've got to learn how to say goodbye graciously as well as hello, and we need rituals to do that, even within our own families. A birthday cake to celebrate a thirteenth birthday doesn't seem to me to be enough, which is why I think the Jewish religion

A THOUGHT ON RITUAL

has it right in making much more of a ceremony out of it.

Anyway, what rituals do you have in your organisation, or in your family? Whatever they are, I should treasure them as a sign of continuity, which is the best basis for change.

47

HOW TO SAY THANK YOU

THE OTHER MORNING a letter arrived at my cottage in the country. It had a very large stamp on it and was addressed only to 'Professor Charles Handy, England', but our redoubtable postal service tracked me down, and there it was.

So I opened it and a letter came out. All it said, in rather scrawly handwriting, was: 'Dear Charles Handy, thank you so much.'

There was no return address and I couldn't decipher the signature. So if it was you who sent it, thank you so much. You made my day. Forgive me for not replying, but I couldn't read your name.

'Thank you.' Two little words, but they mean so much.

That afternoon I went to the supermarket to do some Christmas food shopping for the family, and was somewhat staggered by the huge sum of money I was offering up my bank card to pay.

HOW TO SAY THANK YOU

I said to the lady at the till, 'Look at that amount. You might at least say thank you.'

'I don't need to,' she replied. 'It's on the receipt.'

OK, you might think. But the trouble is, those two little words mean nothing unless they are accompanied by two names: that of the thanks-giver and that of the receiver.

Her late Majesty the Queen, dishing out medals at the Palace, was always careful to thank people by name for their service. It made all the difference. Otherwise, those two little words are just chaff in the wind, or words on a receipt.

We should use them more often. They cost nothing yet mean so much. But please, where possible, always attach a name.

48

WHO IS GOD?

THE HERO OF this story is a little girl in south India. I have no idea what her name is or anything about her and I hope the story is true because it deserves to be, it is so sweet. But I found it in an old copy of *Reader's Digest*, so I can't promise that it is more than a fable.

The little girl, aged seven or eight, was at the back of the class in her primary school in Kerala, scribbling away, when her teacher said to her, 'What are you doing, child?'

She said, 'I'm drawing a picture of God.'

The teacher said, 'Don't be silly, no one knows what God looks like.'

'They will do in a minute,' said the little girl, 'when I've finished this,' and closed her exercise book.

What self-confidence, what bravura. In that great poem 'Invictus' by William Henley, the last two lines read:

WHO IS GOD?

I am the master of my fate:
I am the captain of my soul.

This little girl, who could neither read nor say those words, absolutely embodied them.

I am ashamed to say that if I had been the teacher I would, in order to widen their horizons (but also to impress the class), have whisked them all off to Rome, to the Vatican, to Michelangelo's painting on the ceiling of the Sistine Chapel, where he portrays God as a not very friendly old man. They probably would have been impressed but they would have learnt very little, unless I had related it to their own experience.

I am fond of misquoting Alexander Pope when I say, 'education is experience understood upon reflection'. We can help with the reflection but we can't give the experience. That's up to the students.

I spent three years at the Massachusetts Institute of Technology in Boston being lectured by some of the great names in Economics and Psychology, but to be truthful, the only things I remember are the essays I wrote myself, interpreting my own experience.

Education is about drawing out of people what they already know but don't understand, not putting in what they will forget immediately.

I have to remind myself of that when I give lectures.

Perhaps it's just as well that I don't address primary school classes, but only middle-aged executives who are too immersed in their own lives to want to talk about anything else anyway.

But back to the little girl in Kerala. I wonder what she drew in that exercise book. Was it her daddy, or maybe her mummy? Or did she draw a picture of a king, sitting on a cloud perhaps, with a crown on his head?

But you know what? I suspect what she drew was a picture of her teacher. Certainly that would have been true of our home in south-west London if I'd asked my little daughter, at the age of seven, to draw a picture of God. It would definitely have looked like Miss Goddo, her form teacher. Miss Goddo had the equivalent of papal infallibility and certainly outranked me, a mere professor at the London Business School.

When at mealtimes my daughter said, 'Miss Goddo says . . .' I would brace myself, for I was about to be told that Miss Goddo disagreed with something I had said. And Miss Goddo certainly knew the word of God.

And I am very grateful for her. Because she drew out my daughter's imagination and provided her with a sort of guide rail up the hill of learning, of life, to cling on to if needed.

When she eventually died, we were all bereft.

There is an inscription on the wall of the oldest

working classroom in the world – which happens to be in Eton College, where you can still sit on the same benches as they did in the sixteenth century – which says, in Latin but I will translate, 'It is the job of the teachers to bring out the genius that is in each pupil.'

Find the genius in anybody in the classroom. That's the job of the teacher.

Luckily, my teachers found it in me, such as it was, and that changed my life.

In fact, the course of my life has been dictated by people who expected more of me than I thought I could deliver, but believed I had the capacity to do it. In a sense that's what management and leadership is all about: finding the gift in others and getting them to use it.

PART 5
LIFE AND DEATH

49

WHAT FUN IT IS GETTING OLD

IT WAS THE weekend of the Jubilee. We planted three trees, and the fridge was full of champagne. My daughter said, 'We don't do enough celebrating in this family.'

'Why – what else should we be celebrating?' I asked.

'Well,' she said, 'what about the fact that you're in your ninetieth year, that you're still alive, and that you're still writing and giving lectures, albeit with different technologies – I think that's pretty remarkable and we should celebrate it.'

'Yes,' said my naughty granddaughter. 'Gaga, why can't we have champagne for breakfast every day for a whole year? That would be lovely.'

'Lovely it might be,' I said. 'But it would make you sick and give me a headache.'

No, I'm not going to celebrate myself. But I'll tell you what I will celebrate: old age.

Most people don't realise what a wonderful stage

of life it can be. Yes, I'm now over ninety and I'm very disabled – sorry, I should have said I have 'mobility issues' – so I can't walk very much, which means I'm a prisoner in my very comfortable home and the Norfolk countryside.

I can't go anywhere outside without an escort, preferably in motorised transport, but otherwise in my private carriage (also known as a wheelchair), often propelled by my grandchildren.

But I live like royalty. I don't do anything for myself: if I lift a finger, somebody runs to ask what I want. I have a delightful young woman, a British citizen from Zimbabwe, who cares for me. She dresses me and undresses me, cooks for me, makes sure I take my pills, etc.

Just like royalty in fact. What is there to complain about? I'm well fed. Apart from my mobility issues, I'm well. I have no pain. I'm catching up on my reading. Like Nero, who played the lute while Rome burnt, I watch a country descend into chaos while I listen to Mozart.

I'm a sort of passenger these days – a voyeur of society. I feel guilty about that but then I think that I'm too old to be of use to anybody, so I might as well sit back and enjoy life – which is exactly what I'm doing. I probably eat too much. My carer allows me to have a little wine with meals. I watch too many films on television. I try not to watch the news – too depressing.

What's not to like?

Of course, I recognise that old age can be a very difficult time for many, that I am very fortunate. My point here, though, is that the immutable sense of mortality that goes with it should not in itself be a cause for sadness. For the moment I live each day, not as if it were my last, but as if there were quite a few more to come. The time I have left is of course getting less and less, so I must enjoy every day while I can.

I look out at a lovely scene. The sun is shining most days at some stage. I can't walk far unaided but, amazingly, I lift myself out of my chair to do a little 'jog' around the garden, every day after breakfast, just to show I still can.

I can wear whatever I like, whatever the occasion, and nobody objects. I can forget what day it is and people just think to themselves, 'Old men forget, poor old boy.' But they don't complain.

People listen to my more extraordinary ideas and think I'm some kind of wise man, which of course I'm not, but age gives you this sort of assumed authority which people seem to revere. So why not take advantage of it?

Here I am sitting in the most beautiful countryside,

indulging myself in all the things I love to do. It's a fantastic time of life. As my son said the other day, 'If this is what old age is like, I can't wait to be old.'

So let's celebrate old age. One way I do this is by performing a daily ritual inspired by Lewis Carroll's wonderful nonsense poem 'Jabberwocky'. In it, when a man discovers his son has killed the Jabberwock, he breaks into a celebration:

> *'And hast thou slain the Jabberwock?*
> *Come to my arms, my beamish boy!*
> *O frabjous day! Callooh! Callay!'*
> *He chortled in his joy.*

Every morning when I wake up, I shout out to my astonished neighbours (who are probably too far away to hear anyway), 'O frabjous day! Callooh! Callay!' I chortle in my joy. For I am awake and I am alive.

So if you're in your nineties or getting near, may I recommend that you not only copy me, but also read 'Jabberwocky'. In a Looking-Glass world, nonsense can often make more sense than sense.

I promise you, old age can be a frabjous time. Life is good, callooh callay!

50

A LETTER TO GOD

DEAR GOD,

I think I've been working you too hard recently because I've been disappointed in you. Every time I ask for help, nothing comes. When I can't think of an answer, I find myself saying, 'God only knows,' and I'm sure you do but you don't tell me. Or when I stumble and fall once again, I find myself saying, 'God help me from the floor,' but nothing happens. So I'm very disillusioned with you.

In my childhood, you were the one who protected me. You were like a stern headmaster, kindly but stiff and strict. If I kept to your rules, all would be well, but now your rules don't seem to explain to me who I am or what I'm supposed to be doing with my time on this earth. I ask for help but when I pray, I find I'm really just talking to myself . . .

Which actually, on reflection, is fine. I realise that in

theological terms, if you created me in your image, then I am in a sense like you, and so it's up to me to be my own god and take responsibility for my own life. So having been dumping it all on you and being disappointed, I've now reached the conclusion that I was wrong. It is up to me – if I am like you, then there's no one else to talk to except myself. And that's very good. If I'm in the right mood, I can answer my questions quite well.

Why am I here? Because I'm part of the great scheme of things which the Stoics called the *logos* and David Attenborough, in his riveting natural history television series, calls the story of the earth: how everything combines to keep things going so that, yes, spring follows winter and summer follows spring. We are also part of all that because we are needed to make the best of this world, for the sake of the world at the moment; to fight the onset of climate change, to clean up the atmosphere which is killing little children, to slow everything down, to live by nature and close to nature.

At the moment I'm living in Norfolk, in the middle of some fields. And I live by nature. I get up when the sun gets up, I lie down when it goes down. All sorts of weather batters this house and I love it. I sit inside, away from its fury, amazed at the beauty of the trees now standing bare like skeletons, but exquisite in their bareness. And if I get stronger, I hope I will go walking

A LETTER TO GOD

in the woods every morning, and draw both strength and inspiration from the rustle of the leaves in the wind. In the past I would say I was getting close to you. Now, like the Archbishop of Canterbury, I call it my walking meditation, but it comes to the same thing. So yes, the closer to nature, the better I live, and the more useful my ideas are.

I have fallen in love with the Greek philosophers. They didn't talk about God as such or discuss a divine purpose to existence. They said the point of life was true happiness, was the giving of one's best to help others. Or, as I put it, to be the best at what one can be best at, for the sake of others.

In other words, it's no good running a marathon just to beat last year's time – that's not going to do anybody else any good. But if one uses the marathon to get other people to donate to a chosen charity, or a school, then it's being done not just for one's own benefit but for the good of others. You're contributing to the natural world; you're leaving your footsteps on the sands of time. You are in that sense immortal.

To use your language, God, I could say that happiness is actually walking with you and living with you, or in your person of Jesus Christ. But I don't relate to Jesus as well as I do to you. I don't like his pop idol looks. I feel the way people worship him is close to idolatry.

You weren't too keen on that in your wonderful list of Ten Commandments. I do, however, feel I'm in touch with your Holy Spirit and that lifts me up and helps me, encourages me and gives me the strength to think.

So, dear God, I'm sorry to say that I have come to the conclusion that I no longer need you – but to be honest, I also think it's a good thing. I was giving you too much responsibility for my life and I must take it back myself. After all, if you've made me in your image then I should be able to do it. I may not be able to create the world but I can improve it a little, I think, by encouraging the people who run things to do it better, and not to harm the globe as much as they do.

One day soon I will leave this world. I don't know where I will go. I will just disappear into the starry world where I came from. But I will leave something behind, I hope, and that is my immortality.

It was Julian Barnes who said, 'I don't believe in God, but I do miss him.' I used to think that but to be honest, I don't miss you anymore. I am going to do it by myself. But if you can help me, I will be very grateful.

51

INVENTING A NEW LIFE

ARE YOU SOMETIMES dissatisfied with what you've achieved in your life? Certainly, I feel like that. OK, I've sold quite a lot of books – but so what? Most people have never read any of them.

With that in mind, I decided to write the outline of a new autobiography, describing a life I could have had.

I made myself the heir to a beautiful estate in the west of Ireland and I became an MP and a junior minister in a Lib Dem government.

And I was responsible for shepherding through Parliament a new Bill to reshape the constitution, known as the Handy Bill.

In it, the United Kingdom was redefined as a federal organisation made up of the four independent republics of England, Scotland, Wales and (the United) Ireland, each of which elected four representatives to sit in the House of Lords, renamed the Senate.

They were also automatically members of the

European Parliament, thereby ensuring that the voice of Westminster was always heard in Europe.

In due course, I was knighted for my contribution to politics and adequately rewarded financially for my services as a consultant.

So, I lived well and was widely admired as the Handy Bill passed through Parliament to acclaim from all concerned.

I sat back in my chair, well satisfied with my alternative life, which I hoped would be praised by the obituary writers, ignoring my rather pitiful current one.

However, rather like the Wise Men in T. S. Eliot's 'Journey of the Magi', when I returned to where I'd come from, I saw it for the first time. Having created an alternative history for myself, I found on reflection that my current life as an independent commentator on the affairs of the world was much more pleasant than my imagined role as someone trying to shape them.

So I commend you to write your own new life – it might make you more satisfied with your present one. It worked for me, it could work for you.

But I'd still like to see the United Kingdom as a federal state.

52

A POEM TO LEARN BEFORE YOU DIE

PLATO WAS WRONG in some ways but he was also right about many things. And he was particularly right in what he said in 370 BC: that he was worried the invention of writing would stop people using their memories.

When I was a small boy in Ireland, my primary school wanted me to learn a new poem every week. I always chose short ones, but they are some of the best. My favourite poet is another Irishman, W. B. Yeats. I swear that I will learn all his poems before I pass away, starting with 'The Lake Isle of Innisfree':

I will arise and go now, and go to Innisfree,
And a small cabin build there, of clay and wattles made;
Nine bean-rows will I have there, a hive for the honey-bee,
And live alone in the bee-loud glade.

And I shall have some peace there, for peace comes dropping slow,
Dropping from the veils of the morning to where the cricket sings;
There midnight's all a glimmer, and noon a purple glow,
And evening full of the linnet's wings . . .

I find it very calming, and in fact Nottingham Trent University has shown that reading – or, better still, learning – a poem a day is as good as pills for warding off depression. So try it.

If you listen carefully, as they lower me into my grave, you might hear me saying:

. . . I shall have some peace there, for peace comes dropping slow,
Dropping from the veils of the morning to where the cricket sings;
There midnight's all a glimmer, and noon a purple glow,
And evening full of the linnet's wings.

I will arise and go now, for always night and day
I hear lake water lapping with low sounds by the shore;
While I stand on the roadway, or on the pavements grey,
I hear it in the deep heart's core.

If that's heaven, I am happy.

So I recommend, just for fun, a book called *Poem for the Day*, edited by Nicholas Albery with a foreword by Wendy Cope. It features a poem for every day of the

A POEM TO LEARN BEFORE YOU DIE

year by a whole range of poets, from Shakespeare to Kipling, Maya Angelou to Carol Ann Duffy. If you can't quite manage to learn one daily, then at least read one to yourself, slowly, out loud, and ponder. It gets you into 'the deep heart's core'. It certainly gives me great contentment. It drives depression out of the door.

53

BREAKING GOOD

A VISITOR TO the house recently presented me with a beautiful book – very heavy and obviously very special. It was titled *Kintsugi: The Poetic Mend*. I had no idea what that meant.

I opened it and saw photographs of beautiful Japanese ceramics – bowls, plates and vases. Then, as I turned the pages, I noticed that the items had obviously been broken and subsequently mended. Only, they hadn't been mended so as to be 'good as new'. They looked different from what they had once been.

They'd been repaired using the Japanese technique of kintsugi.

In this, the glue that is used to hold the broken pieces together is made from lacquer mixed with gold dust (or sometimes silver or platinum dust).

When the glue dries, the mended item – a bowl, say – is stronger than the original and has visible gold streaks where the breakage points were. Like golden scars.

It isn't the same as the old bowl, but it is beautiful in its own way – often more beautiful than the original. Certainly, the items in the book, with their gold streaks across them, looked very beautiful.

There is a message here for us, say the Japanese. Breakages – events in life that 'break' us – once mended can actually make us stronger and more interesting because they're part of our history.

My late wife loved taking photos of the faces of old people – particularly, I suppose, old women. She said, 'They're so beautiful, they tell you so much. They're like a tapestry, a story of a life revealed on a face.'

Well, I thought that was a bit of an exaggeration, so one morning before I had a shave, I looked at my face. And suddenly I thought, 'Oh my God, what a pitiful thing a man is – and particularly the man I'm looking at. Me. Old, wrinkled and wizened.'

For the first time, I knew what a furrowed brow really looked like. All those parallel lines across my forehead, like a ploughed field – a testament to the endless books I've read and written, my life's work.

What a shame I can't mark the ridges with gold. Then at least I'd be interesting, if not beautiful.

But there it is: a furrowed brow, and bald except for bunches of white hair atop each ear. With other bits of my body failing rapidly too. Soon I'll be like

Shakespeare's old man – 'Sans teeth, sans eyes, sans taste, sans everything.'

Luckily the mirror doesn't show my failing legs and failing arms. Just my now interesting face.

And as I looked at it again, yes, there were tears in my eyes. My long-lost wife, dead now for several years, still missing from my life, and God how I miss her, though she's there in my mind and in my heart, every morning and every night. And the evidence is in my weepy eyes.

My eyes are also weak from looking at too many computer screens for too long. Part of my work.

So yes, mine is a repaired face, a kintsugi face, full of history.

I always say that wisdom is experience understood in tranquillity. And I've had lots of tranquillity in recent times, sentenced to a less active life because of my stroke a few years ago.

And I rather enjoy reflecting on my long life, with its ups and downs and what I've learnt from it. Which I'm bold enough to call my wisdom. Which I hope might sometime be of use to others, if I can interpret it properly.

So yes, my face is a sort of tapestry of my life, as is yours, interesting and beautiful in its way. Particularly if you can get someone to photograph it as well as my wife used to.

BREAKING GOOD

Ernest Hemingway said, 'The world breaks everyone and afterward many are strong at the broken places.'

That is very much the kintsugi philosophy – if you fall, pick yourself up and you'll be the stronger for it, mature from the experience, and your face might show it with a cut or a bruise – but that's what makes it interesting.

If you're a beautiful young creature aged thirteen and your face is flawless, it is also, I'm afraid to say, without much history and without a lot of character.

Get old and worn and you'll be more interesting, particularly if you can reflect on your life in tranquillity. I would go as far as to say that the blessing of old age is kintsugi, the chance to reflect on your breakages and turn them into wisdom.

To be interesting is, in a way, to be beautiful. And I now no longer flinch when I see my face in the mirror each morning. I just say to myself, 'Well, old friend, you've been through it, haven't you? Lucky you to still be alive.'

54

WHAT WOULD THEY WRITE ON YOUR TOMBSTONE?

I ONCE ATTENDED a book-signing event for a distinguished journalist whom I knew slightly. When he saw me coming, he put down his pen and said to me (as well as the surrounding room), 'Ah, Charles – the wisest man I've ever met.'

'Oh, thank you,' I said. 'Could you write that in the book for me?'

'Of course,' he replied.

'Well,' I thought, 'that was a very nice compliment.'

But when we went into the next room where they were serving tea and biscuits, I heard a woman say to my wife, 'Liz, you're the nicest person I know. How do you do it?'

And I suddenly couldn't help getting just a little bit jealous.

So in the car afterwards I said, 'I'd swap wisest for nicest any day.'

WHAT WOULD THEY WRITE ON YOUR TOMBSTONE?

'Well,' she replied, 'you'd better start now – you've got a long way to go.'

I guess that's what marriage can do to you.

But then I thought, 'What adjectives would I like people to use about me to describe how I am in the various areas of my life?'

For instance, as a grandfather, I know my grandchildren would like me to be kind and funny. But 'kind and funny' wouldn't have worked in the organisation I was running. No, as a manager and leader, I wanted to be seen as honest, fair and reliable . . . and, yes, of course, wise.

But then as a husband, well, I can't claim to be physically attractive so I compensate by, I hope, being interesting and, again, reliable and trustworthy.

Same goes for most of my friendships – interesting, reliable, trustworthy. And to strangers, kind and welcoming.

When I went through the list of all my roles in life, two things stood out: one, I needed to work on being kinder or nicer; and two, people needed me to be reliable and trustworthy. It didn't matter how wise I was. That was of no value to them if they couldn't rely on me and trust me.

So it was useful, I think, this self-learning exercise. More of us ought to do it. What adjectives would you like people to apply to you? Perhaps put on your tombstone? *He or she was wise, honest, reliable and kind.*

As I move towards the end of my life, I'm going through a period of self-analysis – and I'm finding that I come up short in so many ways. The question is: what can I do to remedy that? OK, I can do a little 'first aid' in one or two respects, but for the most part I fear I've left it too late. I've wasted some of life in a sense.

However, I hope my children and grandchildren can learn from me. The so-often unsung virtues of kindness, reliability, honesty and fairness are in the end what people remember you for. Not the prizes you won or the money you made or the awards you received.

So why not try my exercise – while you still have a life to live and time to remedy what minor faults you have?

55

THE STOICS AND THE CHRISTIANS

MY CURRENT HERO is Epictetus. He was the great philosopher of the Stoics in ancient ethics. Now the Stoics had an idea that the world was underpinned by what you might call the natural order of things. Just look at nature: spring follows winter which is followed by summer and then by autumn and then things die off in the winter.

So when you look out of a train window and see a lovely green field which will in August turn golden and be absolutely beautiful and then be harvested, turned into wheat and eventually into flour to make us our bread... that is part of the natural order of things.

In Greek the word is *logos*, which is normally translated as 'word', but actually they meant something much bigger: let us just call it 'the natural order of things'. In fact, for short, they called it God, and they'd say, if you want to look at God, look at nature. And look at nature when you want to look at yourself. Everyone is part of the natural order of things.

So, like that wheat field, in due course, your earthly existence will be over. But your time is not yet finished; you have yet to be turned into memories and the stardust from which you originally came. Just like the wheat, which isn't finished until it is reaped and processed, I'm not finished until I am reaped by the great reaper and my words have been turned into memories.

So strangely, a lot of the Stoics were in a sense Christians because they believed that God was represented by the natural order of things. If you look at nature, that is God. And it is amazing. Look at a silver birch tree. It is absolutely lovely but you could not possibly catch its glorious detail even if you were a wonderful painter. Every single leaf is different and yet all the leaves are, in a sense, of a kind, rather like human beings.

In due course, those leaves on the birch tree will turn golden brown and eventually drop off and lie on the pathway beneath, to be swept up and put on the pile to be burnt, just like me. At the moment, however, I am a human being like everybody else but, I hope, in some way, uniquely different. Charles Handy, not John Smith.

I find that quite consoling. And it is funny, I believe, that a lot of the Christian writers were also Stoics or followers of Epictetus. Take St John of the Gospel. If you remember the opening of his account in the New Testament, it is translated: 'In the beginning was the Word and the Word was with God, and the Word was God... All things were made by Him; and without Him was not any thing made that was made.' 'The Word' here is a direct translation of *logos*, but if you retranslate the Greek term as 'the natural order of things', you get: 'In the beginning was the natural order of things, and the natural order of things was with God, and the natural order of things was God and there was nothing that was not in the natural order of things and God.'

And that makes a lot of sense to me. So if I walk in the woods, I am walking with God and that feels very good. The perfection of each leaf and the fact that each leaf is perfect but different and still they are all the same in a fundamental way – I find that very reassuring.

So ponder that today – you are unique as you are one of a kind and you are subject to the natural order of things. Yes, I am sorry, you too will die but you will live on processed into the memory of things by the people who knew you and loved you. That is your after life, that's your new life, that's the end of your proper life. That is what you are there for, part of the natural order of things.

56

PREPARING FOR THE INEVITABLE

YOU FIND WISDOM in unexpected places all the time, I believe. My cleaning lady – sorry, housekeeper, as she prefers to be called – has a standard phrase. It's: 'Never mind.' So when I spill a glass of wine all over the tablecloth, she rushes up to clean it, saying, 'Never mind,' in a cheery voice, meaning, if I interpret her rightly, that it doesn't really matter in the great scheme of things; it can soon be forgotten, passed over. So cheer up and move on.

I find it very comforting, although slightly confusing at times. As when I told her we were moving to live in Windsor Castle where I'd be working with Prince Philip and she said, 'Never mind.' And when I found myself confused over protocol in that strange place, I kept saying to myself, never mind, and it was very reassuring because of course it wasn't consequential, it didn't really matter and, in the great scheme of things, life went on.

PREPARING FOR THE INEVITABLE

There was one time, though, when her usual response took me aback. I had woken up one morning, feeling pretty weak, I must say, and pretty sure that I had a heart attack coming on, which I'd been warned could happen. So when she said to me in a sprightly way, 'How are you this morning?', I said, 'I think it's the day I'm going to die.' And she said, 'Never mind!'

At first I was furious. I had just made the most important statement of my life and she had dismissed it as inconsequential, as just part of the great scheme of things. But then I reflected: 'Well, perhaps she's right, perhaps it is part of the great scheme of things, like the walnut tree I planted fifty years ago, which grew and flourished and dropped its nuts all over the ground, and now is wilting and fading and weakening, just like me, and soon will go. To be replaced one day by another tree, probably not even a walnut. But also welcoming people to our home, at the opening of our courtyard.'

I mean, after all, my passing will not be marked by a public holiday unless the Prime Minister suddenly has a strange notion. Nobody will notice apart from my children and one or two friends. There will be a notice in a newspaper, but life will go on.

At first I found that rather depressing, the thought that everything will happen just as it used to except that I won't be there. But now, as a convinced Stoic, I think that's as it should be. The great events of our life are dictated by the great scheme of things – how we respond to them is up to us, it depends on our character and it shapes our character.

So how do I respond to this new incident in my life? Well, like Hamlet, I think the readiness is all, as he said contemplating his demise: 'If it be not now, yet it will come. The readiness is all.'

I think I am ready, I have done my bit, I hope I did more good than harm. I enjoyed most of it. I've said goodbye to all those I love; I've said goodbye to my favourite view, had a taste of my favourite wine, retired to my bed, and am waiting.

If this sounds at all depressing, let me just say that the days after I thought I was having a heart attack, when I pondered my life and said goodbye to all the people and things I loved, proved to be remarkably pleasant and, yes, enjoyable. Somehow, once you accept the inevitable, it becomes much easier. For one thing, death means no more responsibility. I won't have to worry about anything, even about paying off the overdraft. Somebody else will have to do that. I shall be in a box in the ground, not far from where I'm sitting now in my much-loved Norfolk countryside.

All things come to an end someday – walnut trees, good things as well as bad, my wife as well as others. A

PREPARING FOR THE INEVITABLE

memorial notice somewhere will be all that's left of me, and a few photographs and a few memories. At least on the walnut tree there are walnuts still. I'll just leave some nuggets of silver, I suppose. And a few thoughts.

Goodbye now and make the most of what time you have left, a special time, a time at the end of things.

ACKNOWLEDGEMENTS

WITH THANKS TO those who all, in their different ways, added their good sense and practical experience to my ramblings.

Kate and Scott, my children, for organising my life to grant me the space to think. Tom Hodgkinson from the *Idler* magazine, Nigel Wilcockson, my long-time publisher, Rebecca, Hope and Cathrin (who literally turned my ramblings into text), my dear carers Mark and Margi, and my friend and confidante, Marcia.

A NOTE ON *THE VIEW FROM NINETY*

IN 2019, CHARLES HANDY suffered a stroke. He made a remarkable recovery, but his physical agility was inevitably affected. Rather than type out the essays in this book, as he once would have done, he therefore elected to dictate them and then have them read back to him for comment. Readers familiar with Charles's previous works may detect an occasional lack of final polish in some of these pieces that reflects the way in which they were produced. The ideas expressed, though, remain engaging and fresh – the fruits of a mind that continued to be active and curious until the end.